Praise for *Prophetic*

"This book offers very essential
prophetic ministry. There are many books available that deal with the subject of prophetic ministry, but very few of them offer practical guidelines for how this ministry is to function in a balanced way in the context of the local church. Often, prophecy is used as a means to draw crowds and display a personal ministry, but this ministry of the prophet was given as a gift from Christ to build up the saints and strengthen the local church.

As a pastor of a large church for 44 years, I have found that the guidelines espoused in this book will help to minimize some of "the foolishness" that has been associated with this ministry and eliminate some of the abuses that have led to the hurt of vulnerable people.

It is absolutely vital to the health of local churches that this ministry be released. However, if it is not released in a way that provides proper checks and balances, it can actually cause more damage than good. Part of the problem has been that pastors and church leaders have not had a systematic way to integrate the prophetic ministry into the life flow of the church. This book will give leaders a framework to do just that.

Prophetic gatherings in the local church can be the highlight of the congregational experience. I do not believe there is any greater, emotionally impacting meeting than a service where the people of God gather with fasting, prayer, teaching, and a release of prophetic ministry. This book offers practical wisdom for church leaders to ensure that the local church receives the full blessing and benefit of such ministry."

—DICK IVERSON

Founder/Chairman, Ministers Fellowship International

"*Prophetic Gatherings in the Local Church* is an impressive, comprehensive study of biblical prophecy. It seems to leave no stone unturned in answering the important questions about prophecy. The explanation of why and how to have a prophetic presbytery in the local church is particularly good."

—ERNEST GENTILE

Author & Prophetic Minister, Founding Pastor, Christian Community Church

"Brian Daehn has blessed the Body of Christ with a thorough scriptural understanding of the fourth major doctrine of Christ 'the laying on of hands.' There is very little teaching on the doctrine of laying on of hands. There are several purposes of God accomplished through laying on of hands. Brian majors on the ministry of laying on of hands with prophecy in a prophetic presbytery.

I received prophetic presbytery from the presbyters at the Bible college I was attending in 1953. The general preparation and protocol described in this book were followed. These are suggested guidelines for a prophetic presbytery in a local church. The detailed directives given would not be applicable to the ministry of an individual mature prophet. Different local churches may vary in their requirements for preparation and participation, but this does not lessen the validity and value of Saints receiving laying on of hands and prophetic presbytery in their local church. This is an essential book for Christians to understand and receive the benefits of the fourth major doctrine of Christ—the laying on of hands and ministry of prophesying."

—Bill Hamon
Founder/Chairman, Christian International Ministries Network
Bishop of Christian International Apostolic Network

"Prophecy is still a mystery to many churches and church leaders. But it doesn't have to be that way. In this timely book, Brian Daehn does a wonderful job of dispelling the fog and clearly showing how biblical prophecy can bless you and your church."

—C. Peter Wagner
Chancellor, Wagner Leadership Institute

"Brian Daehn, in his book *Prophetic Gatherings in the Local Church*, has done an incredible job in preparing a textbook for this prophetic generation! Daehn provides both a historical and scriptural basis for the functioning of prophetic ministry. The reader has access to a powerful tool for a greater understanding of the development of prophetic ministry in an individual's life as well as the release of prophecy in the local church.

I highly recommend *Prophetic Gatherings in the Local Church* for anyone desiring to be used by the Lord in prophetic ministry. I also encourage pastors and ministry leaders to use this valuable book to help steward the prophetic ministry in your gatherings. *Prophetic Gatherings in the Local Church* is destined to help shape the Church for greatness in the days ahead!"

—Barbara Wentroble
Founder, International Breakthrough Ministries

PROPHETIC GATHERINGS in the Local Church

The Laying on of Hands & Prophecy

BRIAN DAEHN
with David Blomgren

PROPHETIC GATHERINGS IN THE LOCAL CHURCH

The Laying on of Hands and Prophecy

ISBN 0-9724320-1-9

Cover design by alphacreative.com
Interior design and typeset by Katherine Lloyd, The DESK

Christian Life Publishing
2706 NE 164th Ave. • Vancouver, WA 98684
www.ChristianLifePublishing.org

Printed in the United States

NOTE

The reader will note on page 18, paragraph one, the transliterated English spelling for the Hebrew word for "hand" as being *yadh*. There are no absolute rules of transliteration, but since most current commentaries and word study books transliterate this word as *yad*, it has been decided to update this book and change the spelling in future editions to *yad* throughout the book wherever *yadh* had previously been printed. It is hoped that this explanation will be helpful to the reader as understanding is sought on this important subject.

Table of Contents

SECTION TWO: PROPHECY

SECTION THREE: PROCEDURES OF A PRESBYTERY

Foreword

Today throughout the nations of the world God is fulfilling His word which he spoke through the prophet Joel many years ago. This prophecy was that in the Last Days, God would pour out His Spirit upon all flesh (Joel 2:28). The outpouring of God's Spirit would result in people having dreams and visions, and both men and women would prophesy (Acts 2:17–18).

Prophecy is such a powerful and essential gift to the Church. Yet some people because of either lack of knowledge, improper motives, or selfish desires have caused harm to the Body of Christ by the use of this gift. Others have used this gift outside the local church with no accountability or oversight and have caused even more problems. The results are that some people reject prophecy altogether, while others receive anything and everything from a so-called prophet. Both of these are unwise responses.

This book, originally written by my father in-law (Dr. David Blomgren) is indeed a classic on prophetic ministry in the local church. This book that you are about to read will instruct you biblically how, when, and why prophetic gatherings should take place in local churches. When prophetic ministry is conducted in a godly, biblical manner under proper local church authority, the blessings that God had intended this ministry to have will continue to endure year after year. I have had the pleasure of ministering for well over a decade in prophetic presbyteries all around the world, and have seen the blessing of prophetic gatherings in many local churches.

In these last days, as we seek to bring the Church back to the power and influence we have seen in the Book of Acts, we must receive and release the ministry of God's holy prophets to our congregational gatherings. This book will continue to serve as a wonderful blueprint for prophetic gatherings for many, many years to come. I encourage all pastors and leaders to read, learn, and implement the material in this book so that we can all enjoy the wonderful blessings that God intended us to have in our churches through the ministry of the laying on of hands and prophecy. My desire is to continue to instruct, equip, and father many 21st century prophets who will build, strengthen, and comfort Christ's Church in these last days. Please join me in this task and let us embrace prophetic gatherings in our local churches today. Thank you David for your wonderful contribution to the Body of Christ through the many hours of research and study you've put into this book. I have updated these truths to reach another generation of believers and ministers.

—Brian Daehn

Introduction

In this day God has truly been pouring out His Spirit on all flesh. Many sons and daughters are prophesying as Joel foretold (Joel 2:28). Numerous gifts of the Spirit and ministries are now operating in the Church. Each believer in a local church has a responsibility to be a "joint that supplies" (Ephesians 4:16).

It is necessary that these ministries be commissioned, confirmed, and set in order in each local church. It is the ministry of the presbytery with prophecy and the laying on of hands which God has ordained to fulfill this vital need.

Prophecy and the laying on of hands of the presbytery was practiced by the early church (1 Tim. 4:14; 2 Tim. 1:6). The Holy Spirit spoke through New Testament prophets in bringing direction and guidance (Acts 13:3). Spiritual gifts were imparted and confirmed through the prophetic word and the laying on of hands (1 Tim. 1:18).

Soon, however, the prophetic ministry began to vanish. The church, which once was persecuted, now became popular because of the legalization of Christianity in the fourth century by Constantine. The result was a decline of spiritual power in the church. The gifts and ministries of the Holy Spirit ceased to operate, and the church was plunged into the Dark Ages. The laying on of hands and the presbytery became only a ritual.

Since the time of the Reformation, however, God has been restoring divine principles and truths that were believed and experienced by the early Church. At the beginning of this century, spiritual gifts began to be restored. God has likewise been restoring to the church prophecy and the laying on of hands of the presbytery. It is no longer a mere form nor an empty ritual, but it is again that through which God gives impartation, direction, correction, confirmation, and blessing.

THE NEED FOR THE STUDY

Soon after God began to restore prophecy and the laying on of hands of the presbytery to the Church, abuse and misuse of this ministry by some brought a critical rejection of it by others. Lack of teaching and lack of careful, biblical guidelines in some quarters in exercising this ministry was responsible for bringing a reproach upon it. The reaction of some to completely reject this ministry rather than bring it into proper balance was itself an extreme.

God has been raising up mature ministries who are ordained of God to be apostles and prophets. These ministries are functioning in this ministry with the wisdom of God unto edification of the churches. There is need, however, that further teaching be continually made available on this biblical practice. It is not the purpose of this study to be a final "last word" on this subject, but only to contribute as an additional resource for this area of truth.

THE PLAN OF THE STUDY

This study assumes several critical propositions, the most important being that of the verbal, plenary inspiration of Scripture. The biblical record is the determinative source for our investigation and the sole criterion for our conclusions. Tradition, expediency, or even popular demand cannot govern our considerations in the function of presbytery meetings.

A presbytery meeting involves the following areas: (1) the laying on of lands; (2) prophecy; (3) a presbytery; (4) the local church. The order of this study will follow these obvious divisions. It will comprise three major sections: Section I—The Laying on of Hands; Section II—Prophecy; Section III—Procedures of a Presbytery.

The general method of inquiry will be to determine inductively from Scripture the biblical content for each of these areas and to synthesize it into a structured framework of truth.

- *Section One* -

The Laying on of Hands

THE HISTORICAL SYNOPSIS OF LAYING ON OF HANDS

Historical Background

The laying on of hands was a familiar practice as early as Patriarchal times. The first biblical instance is that of Jacob laying his hands upon the two sons of Joseph, Ephraim and Mannaseh (Gen. 48:13–22). The Book of Job, which should be dated in Patriarchal times, also mentions this practice. A judge (daysman) would place his hands on the heads of disputing parties so as to impose his authority on both to express his power to adjudicate between the two persons (Job 9:33).

This biblical practice was soon corrupted at a very early time among the heathen. Ancient cuneiform writings from Mesopotamia record this practice of laying on of hands. In Babylonia, healing of the sick was effected by laying the hand on the head of the sick person. The Babylonian king would annually seize the hands of Marduk, a Babylonian idol god, and by this procedure renewed his royal dominion for the new year.

Ancient Eastern literature spoke of an overabundance of energy in a healthy person which could be transferred to the sick by the laying on of hands. In Sanskrit, this concept was described by the word *prana*, which meant "vitality or vigor." The sick person was viewed as having a deficit of *prana*.

Egyptian hieroglyphics portray this practice, and it is often depicted on Egyptian monuments. These records picture the blessings of the gods being conveyed to new Egyptian Pharaohs by means of the gods laying their hands on them. By this means there would be conferred upon them a long life and glorious reign over Egypt. Also, the myth of Isis portrayed the goddess as laying her hands on a dead child who was then brought back to life.

Among the Hebrew people the laying on of hands was a vital part of the Levitical sacrifices and offerings. Laying on of hands was practiced as well as confined to the blood offerings unto God. In this regard it first appeared in Leviticus 1:4 for the burnt offering, then in Leviticus 3:2 for the peace offering, in 4:4 for the sin offering, and in Leviticus 16:21 for the scapegoat of the Day of Atonement. Laying on of hands is mentioned in respect to all the blood offerings, with the exception of the trespass offering. This exception was probably because of the close similarity between the sin and trespass offering. Both of these offerings were for an appeasement to God for the transgressions of the offerer.

The laying on of hands meant more than a mere declaration that the sacrificial offering was indeed the property of the officer, showing his right to offer it to God, as some have maintained. If this was the case, then hands would have been expected to be laid upon bloodless offerings as well. Such offerings were just as much the property of the offerer as were the animal sacrifice offerings.

Witnesses were directed to lay their hands upon a blasphemer (Lev. 24:14) or an idolater (Deut. 17:7), thereby appointing him to death. Laying on of hands was also used to ordain ministry. It was practiced in the ordaining of Aaron and his four sons (Ex. 29:1–28), and the ordaining of the Levites (Num. 8:5–22).

In the New Testament the laying on of hands was likewise practiced in the commissioning of ministry. Thus it was used to commission deacons (Acts 6:1–6), to ordain elders (1 Tim. 5:17–22), and to send forth various ministries (Acts 13:3). Laying on of hands was also practiced to minister healing (Mark

16:18), to minister the Baptism in the Holy Spirit (Acts 9:17), to impart spiritual gifts (2 Tim. 1:6), and to impart blessing (Matt. 19:15). These aspects of laying on of hands will be further developed in a later chapter.

In the post-apostolic church, laying on of hands continued to be universal in practice. Many of the early church fathers were witness to this fact: Irenaeus (died 202 A.D.), Adv. Haer, Bk. II, 4; Theophilus Antiochenus (170 A.D.), Ad. Autol. 1. i. c12, al.17; Tertullian (200 A.D.), De Bapt. c. viii, De Resurr. Carn. c. viii; Clement of Alexandria (200 A.D.), Apid. Eusebius 1. iii. c. 17; by Origin (250 A.D.), Hom. vii in Ezek.; Cyprian (250 A.D.), Ep. pp. 70,73; by Firmillian (250 A.D.), apud. Cypr, Ep. p. 75,78; Cornelius (260 A.D.), apud. Eusebius 1. vi. c. 43. Indeed almost all of the major post-apostolic fathers of the fourth and fifth centuries make mention of the practice of the laying on of hands as functioning in their day.

As mentioned above, the Dark Ages saw this practice become a meaningless ritual, devoid of power and without the prophetic accompaniment. As God began to restore that which was lost by the early church, it was to be expected that this ministry would likewise be restored to the church. It began to be restored around the middle of the 20th century.

The Hebrew Concept of Laying on of Hands

The Hebrew concept of laying on of hands involved the imposing upon the object a responsibility and obligation. The Hebrew word always used in the Old Testament for the "laying on" of hands was *samak*. This Hebrew verb, as the rabbis pointed out, meant more than simply placing the hand upon the object. It meant to lay the hand so as to lean heavily upon the victim.[1] It conveyed the idea of forcibly "pressing down" upon the object[2] so that the victim was viewed as being a "support, sustaining, or upholding" the one who laid hands upon him.[3]

This sense of the word is illustrated in the following examples where the same Hebrew word is used:

Psalm 88:7, "Thy wrath *lies heavy* (Hebrew, *samak*) upon me."

Amos 5:19, "...and *leaned* (Hebrew, *samak*) his hand on the wall."

Ezekiel 30:6, "Thus saith the Lord; they also that *uphold* (Hebrew, *samak*) Egypt shall fall."

Thus the victim had forcibly pressed upon him the physical weight of the one laying on his hands. The object of hands imposed must support the weight of that which was laid upon him. This conveyed the idea of the pressure or weight of responsibility which was to be borne by the victim by the laying on of hands. He must now bear an obligation because of the laying on of hands which was not his before.

In the Levitical offerings there was an impartation to the victim of sin and obligation to suffer for sin. There was in the laying on of hands a transference of guilt and blame for which the victim was now held responsible. Thus there was imposed upon the object by hands laid upon him an obligation to support the weight of that responsibility.

As it will be seen later, the laying on of hands and prophecy by a presbytery likewise conveys a weight of responsibility and obligation upon the candidate. This is not a liability for sin of guilt or blame as with the sacrificial offering, but rather a new responsibility is laid upon him as a weight to fulfill the prophetic word which has come to him.

The Greek Concept of Laying on of Hands

The Greek concept of laying on of hands, as conveyed in the Greek verb, was that of *contact* by means of which a channel was provided for transmission from one to another. The Greek word for "laying on" of hands is *epitithemi*. As a verb, it is found 270 times in the Septuagint and 42 times in the New Testament. Of the New Testament usages the verb is used 20 times in the sense of "laying on" of hands and also 4 times in this sense in the noun form.

This Greek verb is a compound form composed of the preposition *epi* prefixed to the verb *tithemi*. This preposition, *epi*, has the sense of something being *upon* something else.[4] When prefixed to a verb (i.e., called the perfective use of the preposition) as with this form, it bears the idea of physical contact or touch. Thus the verb *epitithemi* has the idea of a putting or placing upon the object so as to touch or come in contact with the object.

The Greek *papyri* also carried this sense of the word. A *papyri* fragment from the second century A.D. speaks of "the seals which he *affixed*." The word "affixed" is the same Greek verb, *epitithemi*, bearing the idea of contact.[5]

This Greek concept, as seen in the Greek verb, therefore, emphasizes the aspect of contact and touch in the laying on of hands. There is an identification with the object by means of this contact. The contact of anointed hands becomes the channel through which something is transferred to another.

THE SCRIPTURAL SIGNIFICANCE OF "HANDS"

The usage of the word "hand" in Scripture brings vital significance to bear upon our understanding of the doctrine of laying on of hands. The word "hand" is used by the biblical writers to describe that which is associated with vast power, authority, strength, and might. The concept of power in the hands is an intrinsic idea which is deeply embedded in the Hebrew language. The most widely used of the original words for "hand" in Scripture is the Hebrew word "yadh." This Hebrew word is derivative of the Assyrian word "idu", meaning "strength." Thus, it may be seen that the concept of power and strength is inseparable with the idea of the hand. The laying on of hands would be seen as that which draws from a reservoir of great strength.

The word "hand" is also used as a term which speaks of placement, borders, setting within certain boundaries or within prescribed dimensions. It also is a term for ministry or preparation for ministry.

Thus the term "hand" is associated with power in the hand, placement within boundaries, and preparation for ministry. As we will see later, these meanings describe the function realized in the doctrine of the laying on of hands.

Scriptural Terms for "Hand" in the Original Languages

The original languages use the word "hand" in a wide range of meanings. Three different terms are used in the Old and New Testaments for "hand." They occur approximately 2,000 times in Scripture by biblical writers.

Hebrew Words for "Hand"

Yadh. This Hebrew word is found 1,606 times in the Old Testament. There are over 80 different words in the King James Version which are used to translate this one Hebrew word. The multiple meanings which this word conveys has great significance.

Kaph. This Hebrew word is used only 190 times in the Old Testament. It bears the idea specifically of the palm of the hand.

Greek Words for "Hand"

Cheir. This Greek word is found 179 times in the New Testament. It has inherited a variety of idiomatic expressions through the Septuagint from the Hebrew words for "hand."

Cheirotoneo. This second Greek word, although not a direct term for "hand," is an important related word. It is found only twice in the New Testament, Acts 14:23 and 2 Corinthians 8:19. This term is a compound Greek form of the word for hand, *cheir*, and the word meaning "to stretch," *teino*, thus having the idea of stretching forth or extending the hand. The word is used in both passages as descriptive of the commissioning of ministry through the stretching forth and laying on of hands.

The Usage of the Term "Hand" in Scripture

The "Hand" is Used as a Term Denoting Power

The "hand" is a term synonymous in Scripture with vast power and might. This concept is the most frequently found sense conveyed by the biblical writers. This power is both realized in the exercising of the "hand" and is also seen as a power which is within the hand. There are four different ideas conveyed by the word "hand" as a term denoting power.

a. Power by the use of the hand

Exodus 14:31, "And Israel saw that great *work* ("hand," *yadh*) which the Lord did upon the Egyptians: and the people feared the Lord." Here the great deliverance of Israel and the destruction of the Egyptians is described by the exercising of the "hand." Notice also Exodus 13:3, 9, 14, 16 where the phrase "by strength of hand" is repeatedly used (obviously in the appositional sense) to convey the sense of vast power instrumental in the redemption of God's people from Egypt.

Deuteronomy 34:12, "And in all that *mighty hand*, and in all the great terror which Moses shewed in the sight of all Israel." Here the hand bears such a concept of might in its use that it brings "great terror."

Job 5:20, "In famine he shall redeem thee from death: and in war from the *power* ("hand," yadh) of the sword." Here the term "hand"is used to convey the sense of potential destructive power of a sword when wielded (cf. Ezekiel 35:5).

Isaiah 28:2, "Behold the Lord hath a mighty and strong one, which as a tempest of hail and a destroying storm, as a flood of mighty waters overflowing shall cast down to the earth with the *hand*." Here Isaiah gives a vivid, hyperbolic description of the power of the hand which can cast down Ephraim, described as also "mighty and strong." The descriptive imagery of the power of the hand is compared to a hail storm which brings great destruction and a mighty flood of waters.

b. Power within the hand

The word "hand" is often used in the sense of potential power which is resident within the hand itself. The use of the term "hand" in these passages is mostly metaphorical.

Deuteronomy 32:36, "For the Lord shall judge His people and have compassion on His servants, when He sees that their *power* is gone, and there is no one remaining." The word "power" is the Hebrew word for "hand," *yadh*. The hand is used here in the sense of that which would be expected to have power and strength "shut up" or stored within it.

Psalms 22:20, "Deliver my soul from the sword; my darling from the *power* ("hand," *yadh*) of the dog." The "hand" of the dog is a metaphorical description of resident power within the enemy himself.

Psalms 49:15, "But God will redeem my soul from the *power* ("hand," *yadh*) of the grave." Here the idea of the "hand of the grave" is that of a latent or static power which is found within the grave, inescapable except for God. (The same expression with the Hebrew word for "hand," *yadh*, is also found in Psalms 89:48 and Hosea 13:14.)

Habakkuk 2:9, "that he may be delivered from the *power* ("hand," *kaph*) of evil." The "hand" is here that which has a power within it to hold a man captive.

c. Security by reason of the power of the hand

John 10:28, speaking of His sheep, Jesus said, "Neither shall any man pluck them out of my hand." Jesus then makes it even stronger in verse 29, "and no man is able to pluck them out of My Father's hand." Here the power of the hand promises a security that cannot be penetrated by any man or force.

Luke 23:46, describes Jesus' dying words on the cross, "Father into Thy hands I commend My spirit." This passage reveals the sense of complete security in which Jesus willingly commended His spirit into the Father's hands.

Isaiah 37:27, "Therefore their inhabitants were of *small power* (literally in Hebrew, "short of hand"), they were dismayed and confounded." This Hebrew phrase, "short of hand," is descriptive of the Assyrians having a state of insecurity. The hand gives the idea of security but to be short of hand is to result in a sense of dismay and confusion on the part of the Assyrians because of a lack of security.

d. Resolution by reason of the power of the hand

Hands are used as a term symbolical of resolve or firm determination.

Judges 9:24, "the men of Shechem, which *aided him* (literally, "strengthened his hands") in the killing of his brethren." The phrase "strengthened his hand" means that they made King Abimelech more resolved to kill these men. Here the hand is that of firm resolve in its meaning.

Psalms 76:5, "The stouthearted are spoiled, they have slept their sleep: and none of the men of might have found their hands." The idea of losing or finding the hands has to do with the matter of firm resolve. Here, those who are described as spoiled and lethargic have lost their purpose and resolve, and thus they have not "found their hands."

The "Hand" is Used as a Term Denoting Authority

The "hand" is also used in the sense of authority, ruling, or dominion. The sense is that of authority which the power of the hand provides and secures.

First Chronicles 18:3, "And David smote Hadarezer king of Zobah unto Hamath, as he went to establish his *dominion* ("hand," *yadh*) by the river Euphrates." Here the hand is a typical term for authority or rulership.

2 Chronicles 21:8, "In his days the Edomites revolted from under the *dominion* ("hand," *yadh*) of Judah, and made themselves a king." Again we see the hand as typical for authority and ruling of a king.

First Chronicles 25:6, in reference to King David, "All these were under the "hands" of their father for songs in the house of the Lord *according to the king's orders* (literally, "upon the hands of the king"). Here the word "hands" is a term for the authority of King David.

John 5:35, "The Father hath given all things into His (Jesus') hand." This New Testament passage uses the imagery of giving into Jesus' *hands* as descriptive of His authority over all things.

The "Hand" is Used as a Term Denoting Placement

The Hebrew term for "hand" is used also in the Old Testament for placement. It bears the sense of being set within proper boundaries, being set into place, or being set in order.

a. The hand is used as descriptive of sea coasts

The hand is used in the imagery as a restraining hand which holds the bounteous sea water within its proper boundary. It causes the sea to be set in its order of placement.

Numbers 13:29, "and by the coast ("hand," *yadh*) of Jordan."

Numbers 24:24, "And ships shall come from the coast ("hand," *yadh*) of Chittim," Numbers 34:3, "along by the coast ("hand," *yadh*) of Arnon."

Ezekiel 48:1, "the coast ("hand,"*yadh*) the way of Hethlonthe coast ("hand," *yadh*) of Hamath."

b. The hand is used as descriptive of place of location

The hand is used in the sense of proximity to a specific location or a typical term for a place with defined limits. Joshua 15:46, "All that lay *near* (literally, "by the hand of" Ashdod." The hand is used here in the sense of a specific piece of property with defined boundaries.

Isaiah 56:5, "Even unto them will I give in mine house and within my walls a *place* ("hand," *yadh*) and a name better than of sons and daughters." The hand is typical of a location (place) with definable borders or walls.

Isaiah 22:18, "a large country (lit., "large of hands")." In this passage "hands" again define a certain country or land with specific boundaries.

(See also Judges 18:10; 1 Sam. 15:12; 2 Sam. 18:18.)

c. The hand is used as descriptive of a bank of a river

The hand in this usage is also viewed as holding the water within its set place. It is putting the water in its proper place.

Deuteronomy 2:37, "unto any *place* ("hand," *yadh*) of the river Jabbok."

Exodus 2:5, "the river's *side* ("hand," *yadh*)."

Daniel 10:4, "I was by the *side* ("hand," *yadh*) of the great river, which is Hiddekel."

d. The hand is used as a term for "border"

2 Samuel 8:3, "to recover his *border* ("hand," *yadh*) at the river Euphrates."

1 Chronicles 7:29, "And by the borders ("hands," *yadh*) of the children of Manasseh, Bethshean."

e. The hand is used as a term of dimension

In this usage the hand is a typical term for dimension, size or measurement. Genesis 34:21, "for the land, behold, it is large *enough* (literally, 'large of hands')."

The "Hand" is Used as a Term Denoting Strength

There are a number of descriptive phrases which are figurative for the strength of the hand. In these phrases the strength of the hand is viewed as a vital, potential force to be soon realized.

a. The lifting of the hand

The lifting of the hand is an expression of a vow or an oath. The uplifted hand is a pledge that all the strength of that hand will be fully implemented to fulfill that vow or oath.

Exodus 6:8, "I did *swear* (lit., "lift up my hand," Hebrew) to give it unto Abraham."

Deuteronomy 32:40, "For I lift up my hand to heaven and say, 'I live forever.'" Here the uplifted hand is used as a sign of an oath.

b. The putting forth of the hand

• *The commencement of action.* The phrase, "putting forth of the hand," is used in Scripture in the sense of the commencing of some action or activity. The emphasis is on the beginning aspect of that action.

Deuteronomy 15:10, "the Lord thy God shall bless thee in all your works, and in all to which you put your hand."

Deuteronomy 23:20, "that the Lord thy God may bless thee in all to which you set your hand in the land which you are entering to possess." (See also Deuteronomy 28:8, 20.)

• *Healing of infirmities.* The putting forth of the hand is also used in the literal sense for healing.

Matthew 8:3, "And Jesus *put forth* his hand, and touched him, saying, 'I will; be thou clean.' And immediately his leprosy was cleansed."

Mark 8:23–25, "And He took the blind man *by the hand*, and led him and put His hands upon him after that He put His hands again upon his eyes and he was restored, and saw every man clearly." In these instances the putting forth of the hands included the laying on of hands for healing.

c. The shaking of the hand

The shaking of the hand is seen as an act of defiance or a threatening against a foe. The strength of the hand is the potent factor which makes the action a warning.

Isaiah 10:32, "he shall shake his hand against the mount of the daughter of Zion."

Zephaniah 2:15, "everyone that passeth by her shall hiss, and wag his hand."

Zechariah 2:9, "For, behold, I will shake mine hand upon them, and they shall be a spoil to their servants."

d. The stretching out of the hand

The stretching out of the hand is a term in the Prophets figurative for judgment by the strength of that hand.

Ezekiel 25:13, "I will stretch out mine hand upon Edom."

Ezekiel 25:16, "I will stretch out mine hand upon the Philistines."

Zephaniah 2:13, "And he will stretch out his hand against the north and destroy Assyria."

The "Hand" is Used as a Term Denoting Consecration

The consecration of the Old Testament priests is described in Exodus 29:9–36 (cf. Exodus 32:29; 1 Chronicles 29:5). The consecration of the priest qualified him to minister unto the Lord as a priest. The word "consecration" in the Hebrew means "to fill the hands." It speaks of filling of the hands of the priests with sacrifices for the Brazen Altar. A priest who is not properly consecrated before the Lord is viewed as coming before God with empty hands. His hands are not yet ready to be filled.

Exodus 29:9, "and thou shalt *consecrate* (literally, "fill the hands") Aaron and his sons."

(Compare also Leviticus 7:37; 8:22, 28, 29, 31, 33.)

The "Hand" is Used as a Term Denoting Provision

The hand is used in the sense of "opening" of the hand to convey the meaning of provision. The opening of the hand is viewed as an act which provides the supply or provision granted to the individual.

Psalms 145:16, "Thou openest thine hand, and satisfiest the desire of every living thing."

Psalms 104:28, "thou openest thine hand, they are filled with good." The hand in this phraseology is the source of the provision.

The "Hand" is Used as a Term Denoting Ministry

The hand is likewise used as a term synonymous with service to God or ministry. The use of the hand would not be necessarily involved in the ministry, but rather the word would be used as a symbolical term denoting the giving forth of that ministry. The character of the Hebrew language is that of a dynamic nature. Words bear an intrinsic vigor and action within their meaning. Thus ministry would not be understood as an abstract subject but rather as a practical function being given forth.

First Chronicles 6:31, "And these are they whom David set over the *service* ("hand," *yadh*) of song in the house of the Lord, after that the ark had rest."

Second Chronicles 7:6, "And the priests waited on their offices: the Levites also with their instruments of music of the Lord when David praised by their *ministry* (literally, "by their hand," *yadh*); and the priests sounded trumpets before them, and all Israel stood."

Hosea 12:10, "I have also spoken by the prophets, and I have multiplied visions, and used similitudes, by the *ministry* ("hand," *yadh*) of the prophets."

The Use of the Term "Hand of the Lord"

The hand is used in reference to the Lord's hand to convey the following meanings:

a. Judgment

Punitive. The hand of the Lord is a descriptive term which often refers to the judgment of God in punishing the evildoers for their wicked deeds. The hand of the Lord with its mighty power is exercised against the wicked.

Exodus 9:3, "Behold, the hand of the Lord is upon thy cattle which is in the field there shall be a very grievous murrain." The hand of the Lord upon the cattle brings the judgment of disease upon them so that the cattle of the Egyptians die. This is a judgmental plague upon the Egyptians.

Deuteronomy 2:15, speaking of those who died in the wilderness, "For indeed the hand of the Lord was against them, to destroy them from among the host until they were consumed."

Judges 2:15, speaking of God's anger towards His people, "Whithersoever they went out, the hand of the Lord was against them for evil, as the Lord had said."

First Samuel 7:13, "and the hand of the Lord was against the Philistines all the days of Samuel."

To bring Deliverance. Many times the hand of the Lord is exercised both for punitive reasons and to deliver God's people. Other times it is employed for punitive purposes only with no redemptive intention.

Exodus 13:3, "for by strength of the hand the Lord brought you out from this place (Egypt)." (cf. 13:9, 14, 16). Here the hand of the Lord not only was punitive towards the Egyptians but brought deliverance to God's chosen people.

Isaiah 41:20, "That they may see, and know, and consider, and understand together, that the hand of the Lord hath done this." Here the hand of the Lord, although punitive to Israel's enemies, bears an even stronger sense of deliverance.

b. Anointing for the prophetic office

The hand of the Lord is used to convey the idea of the source of anointing which causes the prophetic gift to function. When the hand of the Lord comes upon a man to quicken him, then he can prophesy.

The regular Hebrew word for "anointing," occurring 97 times in the Old Testament, is *mashah*. The root form of this Hebrew word for "anointing" means "to draw the hand over" (someone). Thus we see again the word "hand" associated with the concept of anointing.

2 Kings 3:15, 16, regarding the prophet Elisha, "And it came to pass, when the minstrel played, that the hand of the Lord came upon him. And he said, 'Thus saith the Lord'."

Ezekiel 1:3, "The word of the Lord came expressively unto Ezekiel the priest and the hand of the Lord was there upon him."

Ezekiel 37:1, "The hand of the Lord was upon me, and carried me out in the spirit of the Lord, and set me down in the midst of the valley which was full of bones." Here the hand of the Lord carries the additional concept of bearing a man away in the Spirit so that he may receive visionary revelation.

c. *To bring aid or assistance*

The hand of the Lord is understood as giving help and assistance to God's servants.

Ezra 7:6, speaking of Ezra, "And the king granted him all his request, according to the hand of the Lord his God upon him." (cf., Ezra 7:9, 28). The hand of the Lord upon Ezra brought help and aid in enabling him to obtain his requests from the king.

THE DOCTRINAL SIGNIFICANCE OF LAYING ON OF HANDS

THE FIRST PRINCIPLES OF THE DOCTRINE OF CHRIST (HEBREWS 6:1–3)

The author of Hebrews has just exhorted his readers in chapter five to leave childish things behind and become mature. They have been as children long enough, and they should grow up. Because of their immaturity, they are unable to assimilate the solid food which the writer of Hebrews would like to give them. When they should be already teachers, they still need themselves to be taught "the first principles of the oracles of God" (5:12). This phrase reads literally in the Greek, "certain principles of the beginning of the words of God." The Greek word for "principles" is the Greek word *stoicheia*. This word was used in classical Greek in the sense of "walking in line" and "being in rows." The word came to mean that of "walking in line" by means of the words of God.

In chapter six, verses one through three, the writer of Hebrews describes the six fundamental doctrines upon which Christianity is built. The writer of Hebrews exhorts us to leave "the principles of the doctrine of Christ," literally in the Greek, "the word of the beginning of Christ."

It is important to note that the principles of the "beginning of the words of God" (5:12) as revealed in the Old Testament and the "word of the beginning of Christ" (6:1) as revealed here in the New Testament are the same. These six foundation principles upon which the Christian faith is built are the same in the New Testament as in the Old Testament. Thus each one of these six principles were found in Old Testament practice. 2 Timothy 2:19 states that "the foundation of God standeth sure." The foundation of truth was not altered in the establishment by Christ of the New Covenant.

By exhorting us to "leave" these principles, the writer of Hebrews is not encouraging us to discard them, but rather to build upon them. We must "leave" them as a builder leaves the foundation in erecting his superstructure. The one who continues to lay foundations will never have a finished building. These six foundational areas must be laid down in each believer's life and need not be afterwards repeated.

The chief purpose of all this well laid foundation is that we may "go on unto *perfection*" (6:1), meaning maturity or full growth (the same Greek word here as in Hebrews 5:14, "full age").

One of these six foundational doctrines is the doctrine of laying on of hands (6:2). In the Old Testament the laying on of hands was a commanded ordinance. In the New Testament it is again imperative for all believers as foundational to the believer's spiritual growth.

The Doctrine of Laying on of Hands

The laying on of hands has five distinct functions. These functions are impartation, identification, confirmation, ministration of blessing, and the commissioning of ministry.

Impartation

In the laying on of hands there is an actual impartation that occurs. The one imposing his hands on another brings a spiritual impartation thereby to the one who has hands laid upon him.

a. Scientific evidence of impartation

Secular science has proven that hands impart a force of energy. Medical science has further substantiated this fact. In the late 1960s, a biochemist and enzymologist, M. Justa Smith, did extensive research on the biochemical effects of energy imparted through the laying on of hands. The theory was assumed that if an energy force was imparted during the laying on of hands, that the change would be apparent at the enzymatic level, since enzymes are the crucial factor in the basal metabolism of the physical body. Tests were arranged in which enzyme trypsin solution in several flasks had hands laid upon them for 75 minutes a day. Another flask was exposed to a high magnetic energy field, and a fourth flask was kept untouched in its natural state. The results showed that the two flasks that had hands applied to them demonstrated similar qualitative and quantitative effects to the flask exposed to the high energy field.[6]

Further medical studies by Dr. Delores Krieger, a professor at New York University, showed that the laying on of hands raised the hemoglobin levels in the blood samples of those tested. Pretest blood samples were drawn from all those involved in the testing. It was found that the mean hemoglobin values of the blood samples changed significantly from their pretest value in those that had hands laid upon them while there was no significant difference between the pretest and post-test hemoglobin values of those in the control group who did not have hands laid upon them.[7]

Thus, science has shown that the laying on of hands can bring significant change in the blood level of one having hands laid upon him. This would suggest that even in the natural act of laying on of hands that there is some impartation of life that occurs, since "life is in the blood" (Leviticus 17:13–14).

How are we to analyze and understand this recent research as supporting impartation in the laying on of hands? Is the impartation from hands only a natural phenomenon? Is there only to be considered an imparting of an energy force, effecting the physiological factor of man? Is a study in the laying on of hands to be only a study in the bioenergetics of the human metabolism? The answer to these questions must be an emphatic "no"!

Secular science has provided an invaluable service to biblical truth by supporting and proving statistically what God's Word had purported for several millenniums, that there is an actual impartation which occurs in the laying on of hands. Science, by its essential, empirical nature, could only examine a level of impartation in the laying on of hands that would deal with the physical and material part of man. Man, however, has not only a physical and bodily aspect, but he is also composed of the immaterial, soul and spirit.

God Himself is essentially Spirit and not of a material nature (John 4:24). Therefore, it would follow that the essence of that which God would impart to man through the laying on of hands of His Spirit-filled servants would be more than an impartation of physical energy. Rather it would be expected that God would impart a spiritual vitality, a touch of God's own life.

In Scripture the nature of that which is imparted through the laying on of hands is supernatural in origin. As we will see later, that which is imparted by God through the laying on of hands of Spirit-filled believers is greater than that which could be imparted through natural man. Natural man cannot himself impart through the laying on of hands that which he does not himself possess. He does possess physical energy, and so this in measure may be imparted through hands. But natural man does not have the capability to impart the supernatural, for he cannot impart that which he does not possess, unless it be a satanic counterfeit of one possessed or controlled by Satan. The counterfeit, however, is always inferior to the authentic and true power and manifestation of God.

The impartation of the laying on of hands is also a spiritual impartation. It affects not only the physical, but the soul and spirit as well. A new dimension of supernatural and spiritual impartation through God's empowerment is added to the Spirit-filled believer when he lays hands on another. This dimension is not possible in the natural man.

b. Impartation in the Old Testament

Impartation through the laying on of hands is clearly seen in the Old Testament

- To impart sin to a sacrificial offering.

In the Levitical system the sacrificial offering had hands laid upon it before it was put to death. In the act of laying on of hands there was a transfer to the offering of sin and the obligation to suffer for that sin. The victim stood in the offerer's place, and thus having sin now imparted to it, must be dealt accordingly as guilty and responsible for that sin. A uniform Rabbinical tradition states that it was customary to make a solemn confession of sin at the time when hands were laid upon the sacrificial victim. This was done on the occasion of the scapegoat on the Day of Atonement, and it is also implied in Leviticus 5:5–6 as having been done in the trespass offering.

- The act of laying on of hands was performed by the offerer:

Leviticus 1:4, "And he shall put his hand upon the head of the burnt offering; and it shall be accepted for him to make atonement for him."

Leviticus 3:2, "And he shall lay his hand upon the head of his offering, and kill it at the door of the tabernacle of the congregation" (cf. Leviticus 3:8, 13).

- The act of laying on of hands was performed by Aaron and his sons:

Exodus 29:10 (cf. 15, 19), "And thou shalt cause a bullock to be brought before the tabernacle of the Congregation; and Aaron and his sons shall put their hands upon the head of the bullock" (see Leviticus 8:14 for the fulfillment of it).

- The act of laying on of hands was performed by the Levitical priests:

Numbers 8:12, "And the Levites shall lay their hands upon the bullocks: and thou shalt offer the one for a sin-offering, and the other for a burnt-offering, unto the Lord, to make an atonement for the Levites."

The priests laid their hands upon the victim here because it was the occasion of their own consecration to priesthood:

- The act of laying on of hands was performed by the elders of the congregation on behalf of the whole congregation of Israel:

Leviticus 4:15, "And the elders of the congregation shall lay their hands upon the head of the bullock before the Lord: and the bullock shall be killed before the Lord."

- The act of laying on of hands was performed by the High Priest alone on the Day of Atonement:

Leviticus 16:21, "And Aaron shall lay both his hands upon the head of the live goat, and confess over him all the iniquities of the children of Israel, and all their transgressions in all their sins, putting them upon the head of the goat, and shall send him away by the hand of a fit man into the wilderness."

This account records the Day of Atonement at which time Aaron, the high priest, laid his hands on the head of one of the goats of the sin offering and confessed over him all the transgressions of the children of Israel. The iniquity of the nation was imparted thereby from Israel to the goat. After the sins of the people were transferred upon the scapegoat, the goat was sent into the wilderness. The passage clearly states that their transgressions were "put" upon the head of the goat by the laying on of hands.

- To impart wisdom and honor:

Numbers 27:18–23 describes the ordination of Joshua by Moses. Moses laid his hands upon Joshua (vs. 23) as he was commanded to do. Deuteronomy 34:9 makes it clear that Moses directly imparted wisdom and honor to Joshua at that time through the laying on of hands.

Deuteronomy 34:9, "And Joshua the son of Nun was full of the spirit of wisdom; for Moses had laid his hands upon him: and the children of Israel harkened unto him, and did as the Lord commanded Moses."

- Impartation in anointing:

The Hebrew people believed that there was an impartation to the one anointed with oil. They believed that the anointing act was not only a symbolic gesture but an actual impartation of endowment of the life of God. The Hebrew word for "anointing," *mashah*, meant literally to "smear with the hand." The idea behind "anointing" was that of applying oil in the act of hands laid on the person anointed. This does not mean that every act of anointing involved the laying on of hands, but that the laying on of hands or touch was distinctly associated with anointing. The common belief that by this means there was an impartation further shows the prominence of this concept in the Old Testament.

1 Samuel 16:13, "Then Samuel took the horn of oil, and anointed him in the midst of his brethren; and the Spirit of the Lord came upon David from that day forward. So Samuel rose up, and went to Ramah."

1 Kings 19:16, speaking to Elijah, God said, "and Elisha the son of Shaphat of Abelmeholah shalt thou anoint to be prophet in thy room."

c. Impartation in the New Testament

Impartation in the laying on of hands in the New Testament is seen in four aspects: the ministration of healing, signs and wonders, the Baptism in the Holy Spirit, and spiritual gifts.

1. To minister healing

The ministry of healing through the laying on of hands is much more than a therapeutic touch which transfers physical energy. It is a supernatural impartation of the life of God which brings an instantaneous, complete healing.

The practice of laying on of hands in healing was very prominent in Old Testament times (see above). Indeed Naaman expected this practice in his own healing from leprosy, "Behold, I thought, He will surely strike his hand over the place, and recover the leper" (2 Kings 5:11). This practice was carried over into the New Testament times. The laying on of hands is regularly associated with healing in the New Testament.

Mark 16:18, "They shall take up serpents; and if they drink any deadly thing, it shall not hurt them; they shall *lay hands on the sick* and they shall recover."

Luke 4:40, "all they that had any sick with diverse diseases brought them unto Him; and he *laid His hands* on every one of them, and healed them."

Luke 13:13, "And He *laid his hands* on her and immediately she was made straight, and glorified God."

Acts 28:8, "And it came to pass, that the father of Publius lay sick of a fever and of a bloody flux; to whom Paul entered in, and prayed and *laid his hands* on him, and healed him."

(See Matthew 8:3, 15; 9:18; 20:34; Mark 1:41; 5:23; 6:5; 7:32; 8:23, 24; Luke 22:51.)

2. To minister signs and wonders

The laying on of hands was the channel through which was imparted signs and wonders.

Acts 5:12, "And *by the hands* of the apostles were many signs and wonders wrought among the people."

Acts 14:3, "Long time therefore abode they speaking boldly in the Lord, which gave testimony unto the word of His grace and granted signs and wonders to be done *by their hands.*"

Acts 19:11, "And God wrought special miracles *by the hands* of Paul."

3. To minister the Baptism in the Holy Spirit

In the book of Acts there are three instances of the Baptism in the Holy Spirit being conferred through the laying on of hands (Acts 8, the Samaritans; Acts 9, Saul; Acts 19, the Ephesians).

Acts 8:18, "And when Simon saw that *through the laying on of the apostle's hands* the Holy Ghost was given, he offered them money."

The expression of this passage describes the imparting of the Holy Spirit through the apostle's hands as a fact and the observance of Simon to this fact. This is not stated as only Simon's opinion but rather the fact and Simon's observation of it.

In this passage the Greek preposition *"through (dia)* laying on of hands" denotes a channel of which a process or action occurs. It describes the imposition of hands to be the channel of impartation of the Baptism in the Holy Spirit.

Acts 9:17, "And Ananias went his way, and entered into the house, and putting his hands on him said, 'Brother Saul, the Lord, even Jesus, that appeared unto thee in the way as thou camest, hath sent me that thou mighest receive thy sight, and be filled with the Holy Ghost.'"

Acts 19:6, "And when Paul laid his hands upon them, the Holy Ghost came upon them; and they spake with tongues and prophesied."

There are, in the book of Acts, two recorded instances of the Baptism in the Holy Spirit being conferred without the imposition of any hands (Acts 2 and 10). This raises the question, "Can, therefore, a believer receive the Baptism in the Holy Spirit without the imposition of hands of a Spirit-filled believer? The answer must be affirmative. The laying on of hands are normative in ministering the Baptism in the Holy Spirit, yet Scripture does not confine the reception of the Baptism in the Holy Spirit to this medium as these instances illustrate.

The early church regularly exercised the laying on of hands in the reception of the Baptism in the Holy Spirit. Tertullian was the earliest writer to describe the details of the practices of the early churches. Tertullian writes, "In the next place the hand is laid on us, invoking and inviting the Holy Spirit through benediction."[8]

Cyprian, the contemporary and disciple of Tertullian, also testified to the laying on of hands in the reception of the Spirit baptism as continuing. Jerome and Augustine likewise gave further witness to this practice in their times.

4. To impart spiritual gifts

There is an actual impartation of spiritual gifts through the laying on of hands (see Romans 1:11). The following passages will clearly support this truth.

1 Timothy 4:14, "Neglect not the gift that is in thee, which was given thee *by* prophecy, *with* the laying on of the hands of the presbytery."

Here Paul states that Timothy's spiritual gift was in him "*by* prophecy *with* the laying on of the hands of the presbytery." The Greek preposition "by," is again *dia*, which bears the idea of a direct channel, as mentioned above. Prophecy was a channel through which was imparted a spiritual gift.

The Greek preposition "with," regarding the laying on of hands, is *meta*. This preposition conveys the idea of association and would mean that the laying on of hands was in league with prophecy as a dual means through which was imparted a spiritual gift. Thus the prophetic word and the laying on of hands of the presbytery were both channels through which was imparted the spiritual gift to Timothy.

2 Timothy 1:6, "Wherefore I put thee in remembrance that thou stir up the gift of God, which is in thee *by* the putting on of my hands."

Again the word "by" is the Greek preposition *dia*, conveying the idea of a channel. The laying on of hands was the direct channel through which the spiritual gift was imparted. It is interesting to note that this same word meaning "through" (direct channel) in the ancient Syriac, the sister dialect of the

Aramaic of Galilee, the dialect spoken there by Jesus and the twelve apostles, was ܒܝܕ . This Syriac preposition was a compound form literally meaning, "with the hand of."[9] This same preposition was so used in the sense of a channel of impartation also in the Syriac Peshitta, the ancient and important version used by early Christian believers of the post-apostolic church. Its significance comes from the fact that this version precedes the earliest extant Greek uncials which we have of the New Testament. This further shows that the concept of the hands as a channel of impartation was so prominent that it affected the language of the region near New Testament times.

Romans 1:11, "For I long to see you that I may impart unto you some spiritual gift, to the end ye may be established."

Here we see that Paul was fully aware that he was able through the Holy Spirit to impart spiritual gifts. The above passages make it clear that this was accomplished through the prophetic word and the laying on of hands.

Identification

In the laying on of hands there is also an identification. In the Old Testament Levitical offerings there was an identification of the offerer with the sacrificial victim by means of physical contact. By the laying on of hands, the offerer and the offering became one. The same Scripture passages which convey the idea of impartation in the Levitical offerings also show identification in the laying on of hands (cf. Leviticus 1:4, 3:2, 4:15, 24, 29, 33; 16:21; Numbers 8:12).

In the Book of Job we have another illustration of identification in the laying on of hands.

Job 9:33, "Neither is there any daysmen betwixt us, that might lay his hands upon us both."

This passage describes a "daysman," a judge, who laid his hands on the heads of disputing parties. A day would be set for hearing litigated cases. The presiding judge at the time of the case would lay his hand on each of the two parties. It conveyed the idea of identification. Through the contact of the daysman's hands simultaneously laid on both parties, they became one. There was an identification as one of the parties by the judge as a sign of his mediating between both and reconciling them. The identification showed his full intention to adjudicate between the two persons and bring them into one agreement.

Paul also taught identification in the laying on of hands by giving us a negative warning. In 1 Timothy 5:22 he warns eldership to "lay hands suddenly on no man, neither be a partaker of another man's sins: keep thyself pure." 1 Timothy 5:24 gives us the reason for this warning. Some men's sins are known openly and are dealt with accordingly while some men's sins are secret. Therefore, when we lay hands on someone who is involved in sinful activity, even though secret and unknown to us, there is an identification by the contact with the sinning brother. We become one with the sinning believer and therefore become "partakers" of his sin. Thus we should be careful to know well those to whom we minister in the laying on of hands and the presbytery.

Confirmation

In the laying on of hands there is also an act of confirmation of the one having hands laid upon him. In this regards hands were laid upon individuals, not animals. This confirmation might be of a positive or a negative nature.

In Old Testament times witnesses would lay their hands on those who were accused of a grave offense worthy of death. By the imposition of hands the witnesses were making a formal confirmation as to the guilt of the subject in the offense in question. They thus confirmed the fact that the accused was indeed guilty of this deed.

This is seen in the confirmation by witnesses of the guilt of a blasphemer:

Leviticus 24:14, "Bring forth him that hath cursed outside the camp; and let all that heard him lay their hands upon his head, and let all the congregation stone him."

Also confirmation by witnesses through the laying on of hands is seen in the case of an idolator:

Deuteronomy 17:7, "The hands of the witnesses shall be first upon him to put him to death, and afterwards the hands of all the people. So thou shalt put the evil away from among you."

The scriptural examples of commissioning of ministry (see below) are also instances of positive confirmation in the laying on of hands.

In the Book of Acts there are examples of confirmation: Acts 15:41, "And he went through Syria and Cilicia, *confirming* the churches."

Although it is not directly stated that this confirmation was that of prophecy and the laying on of hands, it is strongly suggested in the two other passages in Acts where this word "confirmation" is mentioned.

Acts 15:32, "And Judas and Silas, being prophets also themselves, exhorted the brethren with many words, and *confirmed* them."

Here it seems clear that the prophetic words had a part in the confirmation of the churches.

The other passage in Acts is in 14:22–23, "*Confirming* the souls of the disciples…and when they had ordained them elders in every church…"

In that laying on of hands was practiced with ordination, it is thus implied that this confirmation may have included as well the laying on of hands.

Ministration of Blessing

There is also a ministration of blessing in the act of laying on of hands. The imposition of hands brings a blessing from God to the ones having hands laid upon them.

Genesis 48:13–20 describes the laying on of Israel's hands upon the heads of Joseph's sons, Ephriam and Manasseh. Jacob invoked a prophetic blessing over each son, crossing his hands so that the younger son, Ephriam, received the greater blessing. It is clearly stated in verse 20 that by the laying on of his hands and a prophetic word, "he *blessed* them that day…."

Blessing is also associated with hands when the hands are not placed directly upon an individual. The lifting up of the hands towards others, which may not bring actual physical contact with them still, is an act of blessing them.

Leviticus 9:22, "And Aaron lifted up his hands toward the people, and *blessed* them…"

Likewise, Jesus blessed those that witnessed his ascension into Heaven:

Luke 24:50–51, "And he led them out as far as to Bethany, and he lifted up his hands, and *blessed* them. And it came to pass, while he *blessed* them, he was parted from them, and carried up into Heaven."

In the Gospels we see the multitude bringing children to Jesus and asking him to lay his hands upon them. This desire for Jesus to lay his hands upon the heads of children originated with the friends and parents of the children, not with Jesus. It shows that the laying on of hands for blessing must have been a regular custom of the time.

Mark 10:13, 16, "And they brought the young children to him, that he should touch them...and he took them up in his arms, put his hands upon them, and blessed them."

The sending forth in ministry in various New Testament instances was accompanied by laying on of hands (see Acts 13:1–3). In this manner the ministry was blessed as they were sent forth to service.

Whereas, the laying on of hands on others was an act of blessing them, so the imposition of hands on one's own head was an expression in Scripture of mourning and sadness.

2 Samuel 13:19, "Tamar put ashes on her head, and rent her garment of diverse colours that was on her, and laid her hand on her head, and went on crying."

Likewise, Jeremiah exhorted Judah to place, "...thine hands upon thine head: for the Lord hath rejected thy confidences..."

Egyptian art also portrayed scenes where the mourner had his hands laid upon his own head in a state of mourning. This action was evidently not only an expression of sorrow but an expression also of the mourner's intent that his circumstances would change and that blessing would now come upon him. It was an act of desiring to bring blessing to oneself.

Commission of Ministry

Laying on of hands was also practiced in the commissioning of ministry in both the Old and New Testaments. The laying on of hands was a vital part of the ordination to the office.

a. Old Testament consecration

Aaron and his sons were the first in Scripture to be consecrated or ordained to ministry in the official sense. The instructions for their ceremony were given in Exodus 29:1–35 and fulfilled in Leviticus 8:1–30. Hands were laid upon the sacrificial offerings used in the consecration ceremony (Leviticus 8:14, 18, 22).

In the consecration of the Levites to priesthood (Numbers 8:5–22), hands were not only laid upon the sacrifices but also upon the Levites themselves by the children of Israel.

Leviticus 8:10, "And thou shalt bring the Levites before the Lord: and the children of Israel shall put their hands upon the Levites."

Thus, by the laying on of hands, the Levites were ordained to "execute the service of the Lord" (Numbers 8:10–11). By this act the people imparted to the Levites the responsibility for the service of the Lord instead of the firstborn of all the tribes. The obligation was transferred from the firstborn to the Levites. The Levites were now to be regarded as substitutes for the firstborn of all Israel. By the hands of the people, the Levites were dedicated and commissioned to special service unto the Lord.

The laying on of hands continued as a regular practice in the ordination of rabbis in Judaism. The practice was used in the commissioning of members of the Sanhedrin in the post-Maccabean period. In Judaism the practice continued as late as the 11th Century A.D.[10]

The commissioning of Joshua to leadership involved the laying on of Moses' hands (Numbers 27:18–23; Deuteronomy 34:9). Moses was directly commanded to lay his hands upon Joshua at this time. This act was not only ceremonial, but effectual in a direct impartation of the spirit of wisdom (Deuteronomy 34:9).

b. New Testament commission of ministry

Laying on of hands was regularly applied in the New Testament examples of ordination, the commissioning, and sending forth of ministry.

- *The Choosing of Deacons.* The imposition of hands was used in the commissioning of Deacons to their ministry (Acts 6:1–7).

  Acts 6:6, "Whom they set before the apostles and when they had prayed, they laid their hands on them."

- *Sending forth of Ministry.* The laying on of hands also was practiced in the commissioning of ministry sent forth.

  Acts 13:3, "And when they had fasted and prayed, and laid their hands on them, they sent them away."

- *Ordination.* The laying on of hands was used in the ordination of Timothy. They were the hands of the presbytery, probably of the Ephesian eldership (1 Timothy 4:14), and also of Paul himself (2 Timothy 1:6).

  Although not directly mentioned, it is obvious that the laying on of hands regularly accompanied all acts of ordination. 1 Timothy 5:22, "Lay hands suddenly on no man…," mentions laying on of hands in a context of a discussion of eldership. In this passage it is a warning to not ordain an elder hastily or without due inquiry and examination. The presbyters or elders would not be expected to practice laying on of hands if they themselves had not received this ministry.

In examining the doctrine of laying on of hands, we have seen through this practice there may be an impartation to the candidate, an identification with the candidate, a conferral of blessing upon the candidate, and a confirmation of the candidate in official recognition of the ministry God has deposited within him and an authoritative recommendation of the candidate to others.

Illustrations of the Doctrine of Laying on of Hands

Scripture has given us varied illustrations of the doctrine of the laying on of hands. While couched and hidden within Old Testament types and pictures, the truth conveyed was divinely intended to illustrate for us the function of the laying on of hands.

Illustration in the Tabernacle of Moses

(Exodus 26:1–37; 36:8–38)

The Tabernacle of Moses consisted of a framework of forty-eight boards of Shittim wood (Exodus 26:15–25). There were twenty boards on the north side, twenty boards on the south side and eight boards along the western end. Each of the boards had at its lower extremity two tenons by which it was connected with two sockets of silver. The tenons extended downward from the board and stood in the silver sockets, firmly taking hold of the sockets so as to allow the board to stand firmly on its foundation.

These boards were once stately acacia trees with their roots in the earth. One day the axe was laid to the roots, and there was a death to the former life. The boards needed yet, however, to be "set in order." They were not to be set upon the shifting sand of the desert which offered no solid base. These boards needed to be "standing up" straight (Exodus 26:15) upon sockets of silver (typical for redemption), but they could not keep themselves standing straight.

It was the tenons that caused these boards to be "...set in order one against another" (Exodus 26:17). The word "tenon" in the Hebrew means "hand." Thus each board was set in order in its placement by the two "hands."

The boards are representative of the believer. The believer experiences a cutting away of the former life and rests upon the foundation of redemption. Yet his life needs to be "set in order" through the "laying on of hands" so that his life will stand straight and be in its proper place in the House of the Lord.

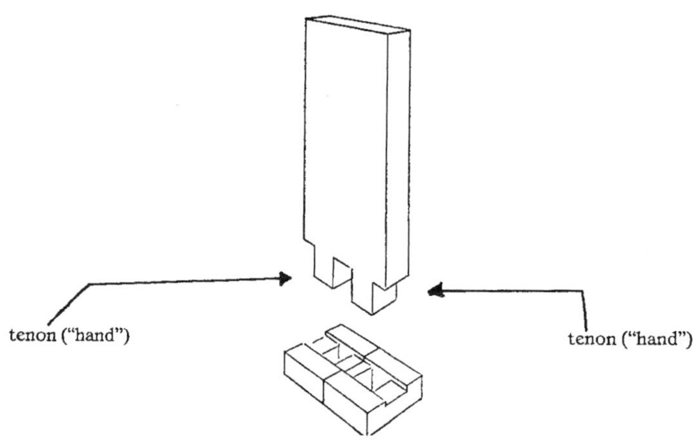

Illustration in the Temple of Solomon

In the Tabernacle of Moses the laver was for the cleansing of the priest. No mention is made in Scripture of instructions for the moving of this Brazen Laver. In the temple, however, there were ten lavers as well as a molten sea (2 Chronicles 4:4–5). This molten sea was for the washing of the priests, replacing the tabernacle laver. The ten lavers in the temple were used for the cleansing of the sacrifices. They were used by the priests to wash the portions of the burnt offerings.

The ten temple lavers had mobile bases which had four wheels operated by a revolving axle. The bases were square chests of brass which served to support and to convey the lavers. These square chests stood upon four feet which were fastened upon the brazen axles and the axles were in turn fastened to the brazen wheels, so as to turn them. The lavers could then be easily moved from one place to another within the court area.

The Hebrew word for "axles" or "axletrees" is the Hebrew word for "hands" (*yadh*). The Hebrew word for "hands" was employed as descriptive of the axles, because God purposed to illustrate the doctrine of laying on of hands.

It was the axles that, as hands, turned the brazen wheels so that the laver might be moved and positioned for greater access in the washing and cleansing of the sacrifices.

The believer as a New Testament priest (1 Peter 2:9) offers spiritual sacrifices to God which must be cleansed and holy to be acceptable and well-pleasing to God (Phil. 4:18; 1 Peter 2:5; Hebrews 13:15–16). Ministry in God's House by the believer is described as spiritual sacrifices. A spiritual sacrifice, however, is only "acceptable" if it is holy (Rom. 12:1).

The fact that in the temple there were ten lavers with their ten axles or "hands" for the moving of the lavers shows how vitally important to God it is to have a cleansed sacrifice. The number ten speaks of divine order. The ten lavers and ten "hands" to move the lavers illustrates the importance of divine order in preparation of sacrifices being cleansed and acceptable to God.

The New Testament church must come under divine order. By the operation of the laying on of hands, as we see illustrated in the temple lavers, divine order is established in the House of the Lord so that there may be greater access provided for the cleansing of the sacrifices. Thus the work of the ministry (Eph. 4:12) in spiritual sacrifices and the worship of God's people (Hebrews 13:15–16) might be acceptable to God.

Biblical history records that wicked King Ahaz later removed the bases with their ten axles and wheels from the lavers (2 Kings 16:17). The bases were eventually broken apart and the brass ruins were carried away into Babylonia (Jeremiah 52:17). Likewise, during the Dark Ages, the doctrine of laying on of hands was separated from church practice and carried away into spiritual Babylon.

Today, God is restoring again the doctrine of the laying on of hands. The ten brazen bases with their axles ("hands") and wheels are being restored to the ten lavers, that there may be divine order for the ministry of spiritual sacrifices, well-pleasing unto God.

Illustration from Judah, the Redemptive Line

In the name "Judah" we see illustrated the significance of the "hand" as an instrument of imparting power and strength.

Judah was the fourth son of Jacob by Leah. Yet he was assigned the responsibilities of the firstborn by reason of the forfeiture of Reuben, Simeon, and Levi because of sin.

Jacob, in his blessing of Judah (Gen. 49:8–12) described him as a mighty man of war whose hand was in the neck of his enemies in triumph. He was as a lion's whelp, ready to spring upon his prey. The sceptre of rule would belong to his descendents until Shiloh came, the Messianic prince.

Moses, in his blessing of the tribe of Judah (Deut. 33:7), prayed that the Lord would hear the *voice* of Judah, and that his hands would be sufficient for him. Here Moses seems to link the thought of the voice lifted to God for help and guidance with the implicit strength and ability of the hands. Judah, the "praise" tribe, would be active in both verbal and manual warfare, both spiritual and natural.

The name "Judah" is a transliteration of the Hebrew word, *yadah*, meaning "praise." This Hebrew word for "praise," from which the name "Judah" comes, is itself a derivative of the Hebrew word *yadh,* the regular Hebrew word for "hand."

Therefore, the root idea behind the name "Judah" is that of the "hand" and the power and strength in the hand. Indeed, Jacob seems to make a pun on this meaning when he speaks prophetically of Judah having his "hand" in the neck of his enemies.

It was this tribe through which God's hand would be made manifest to bring salvation. Judah was destined to be the redemptive line and the tribe through which the Messiah, the Christ, would come. Through Judah, God's hand, there would be imparted He who in power and strength would not only bring deliverance but would bring God's rule.

The Laying on of Hands as a Double Portion

In Genesis 48:13–22, the laying on of hands is mentioned for the first time in Scripture. Here is described the imposition of Israel's hands upon the heads of Joseph's sons.

In the account, Israel put one hand on each of the son's heads, placing his right hand upon the younger son, Ephraim and his left hand upon the elder son, Manasseh. Joseph objected to Israel's crossing of his hands purposely to place the right hand upon Ephraim's head. The younger son, Ephraim, had the right hand placed upon his head because he was to receive the greater promise (48:19) and was to receive the greater blessing.

The objection of Joseph to the right hand placed upon the younger son reflects the Hebrew concept of the right hand bestowing the greater blessing and the left hand bestowing the lesser blessing.

The right hand was conceived of as the place of special honor. Thus to sit at the right hand was to sit in the place of honor (1 Kings 2:19; Psalms 110:1; Eph. 1:20–22). The right hand was also associated in the thinking of the Hebrews with success, prosperity, and righteousness (cf. Isa. 41:10).

The left hand, however, was always considered the lesser, and often it was even associated with evil. In Ecclesiastes 10:2 the wise man's heart is associated with the right hand while the fool's heart is associated with the left hand. In Jonah 4:11 the reference is made to those who could not discern between their right and left hand. In that passage it indicated as an Eastern idiom those who were too young to discern between the good (right hand) and the evil (left hand). In the New Testament, the goats, who are the godless, are placed at the left hand of God as judge, while the righteous appear at His right hand.

The Law of First Reference, however, guides our understanding here in Genesis chapter 48. The left hand in this passage does not imply evil itself but rather that of a lesser blessing. Thus Manasseh has the left hand placed upon his head and received the lesser blessing.

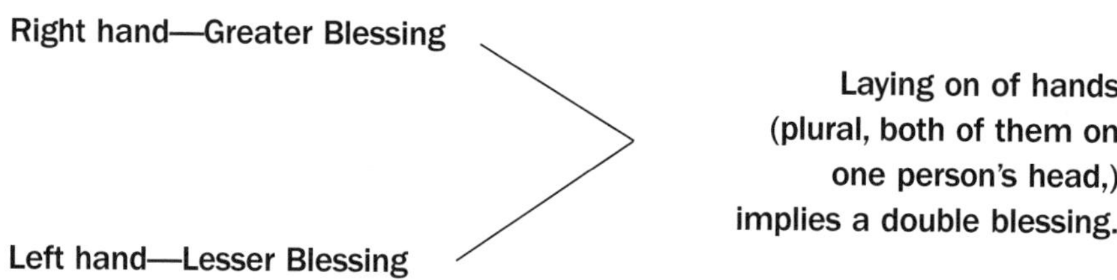

In the account of Israel and Joseph's sons of Genesis chapter 48, as already seen, only one hand is placed upon the head of each of Joseph's sons. Yet there was a distinct blessing imparted through each hand to each son. The doctrine of the laying on of hands (plural, both hands) on one individual denotes a double portion of blessing for that individual.

- Section Two -

Prophecy

Prophecy is obviously an essential part of any presbytery service. Through the prophetic utterance God speaks immediately to those who are presbytery candidates in a specific manner and secondarily to all those present in a general manner. This dual function of prophecy is possible because of the nature of the prophetic word as expressed in divine principles which operate faithfully in accordance with the ways of God. In order for a congregation to benefit most from the prophetic word, it is important to have a general understanding of prophecy and the operation of the prophetic ministry.

THE DEFINITION OF PROPHECY

There are several words in the original Hebrew, Aramaic, and Greek languages of Scripture which are used to designate the prophetic function. A brief study of them will help us to better understand prophecy.

Old Testament Words

There are basically five different Hebrew and Aramaic word roots from which all the Old Testament words for "prophecy" are derived. These five words may be divided according to their meaning into two basic categories. These two categories are firstly, words which emphasize the passive experience of receiving the prophetic message from God and secondly, words which emphasize the active experience of transmitting the prophetic message to the people.

Receptive Function

A distinctive feature of one who would prophesy is that he has received a revelation directly from God. This factor distinguishes him from the false prophet who speaks instead out of his own imagination. Thus, Jehovah says of the false prophets, "I did not speak to them, but they prophesied" (Jeremiah 23:21).

Therefore, the true ministry who prophesies must have received a message from God. Three of the Old Testament Hebrew words are descriptive of this receptive function of the prophetic message.

a. Perceptive aspect

This reception of the prophetic message may be realized in either visionary or perceptive ways.

Ro'eh. "A seer." This Hebrew word occurs 12 times in the Hebrew Old Testament. Essentially the root, *ra'ah*, means "to look at" or "to behold." This word is used of the prophet in his "seeing" or perceiving of God's message, especially, although not exclusively, with reference to the visionary. This word describes distinctively the prophetic revelation of the prophet through visions.

Chozeh. "A seer." This Hebrew word, occurring 16 times in the Old Testament, also denotes the subjective experience of "seeing" God's revealed message. Although these two terms may be used interchangeably, *chozeh* seems to be the broader term and is used to refer to either cognitive or visionary perception.

These two Hebrew terms, both meaning "seer" are synonyms for the word "prophet." First Samuel 9:9 shows that the office of the prophet and that of the seer are identical. The co-equality of these terms is also proven by the constant double usage of them till the latest times. The only distinction in the terms are in function, the "seer" as descriptive of the receptive function and the "prophet" as descriptive of the communicative function.

b. Responsive aspect

This reception of the prophetic message causes different responses in the one receiving this revelation, depending upon the nature of the message.

Massa. "A burden." This Hebrew word occurs 70 times in the Old Testament and most often is translated "burden." It is indicative of the response of the one receiving the prophetic word. The Hebrew root *nasah* may refer to either a burden or weight as a heavy load which is carried or it may indicate the lifting up of the soul.[11]

This Hebrew word is often found in the headings of denunciatory prophetic oracles of judgment. In these passages the grevious and threatening nature of the prophecy seems to have been received as a weight, a burden or load by the prophet who must now in turn deliver this same message of judgment to the people.

This same Hebrew word, however, is also descriptive of the lifting up of the soul in the prophetic flow of the temple musicians as exemplified in the master musician Chenaniah who was master of "song," (Hebrew, *massa,* here a "lifting UP").[12]

Also implicit within this word is the concept that the purpose behind the prophetic word, even when judgmental, is restorative. Even when denunciation is in order because of sin, it is a "lifting up" prophecy, intended to bring them higher in God's ways. Indeed, the main concept behind this word *massa* is that of a lifting up, not a weighing down.

Communicative Function

Hebrew thought commonly presented an idea or an event under two aspects so that the idea or event might be understood in its entirety. The same event may be depicted as divine activity as well as human activity. These various representations would be interconnected and interwoven with each other. Side by side with the representation of God as sovereign in the Old Testament, needing no activity beside himself, the element of human activity assisting God by

God's own choice is also represented. So likewise, prophecy reflects this two-fold aspect in the language of the Old Testament. The prophetic message is at once human activity and divine activity.

Two Hebrew terms are used to describe the communicative function of prophecy. One describes the human activity of the prophet and the other the divine activity of God. The prophetic message is at the same time the words of the prophet and the words of God.

The writer of 2 Kings represented the prophetic function as both the words of the prophet and the words of God, "Now the Lord spoke through His servants the prophets, saying..." (2 Kings 17:13; 21:10; 24:2).

a. The human factor aspect

Naba. "To prophesy." (Also, *Nabiy',* "prophet," Hebrew form; *Nebiy',* "prophet," Aramaic form). This word in the Hebrew and Aramaic forms occurs 114 times in the Old Testament in the verb form and 324 times in the noun form, totaling 435 times in the Old Testament. The greater usage of this word is significant to show the greater emphasis on this aspect of the prophetic office. The prophet was primarily a spokesman for God, whatever the manner in which he received revelation from God.

This Hebrew and Aramaic word *naba* means "to bubble up, to gush forth, to pour forth."[13] This same word is found in the ancient Accadian language as *nabu,* meaning "to call or proclaim," and appears to be the original source for the word.[14] In the Accadian language the element of authority was regularly associated with this word.[15] Thus the original Accadian word conveyed the communicative aspect as associated with authoritative proclamation. The latter Hebrew derivation reflects further the influence of the divine activity upon the human personality as the prophetic message "bubbles up" and "gushes forth" as a mighty torrent from the prophet's lips.

Some consider the Hebrew derived meaning of "bubbling" and "gushing" as denoting an ecstatic aspect in prophecy.[16] However, it is better to see this as the human activity of the prophet in response to the anointing hand of God upon the prophet. Thus the prophetic message pours forth from the anointed prophet as water from a fountain.

b. The divine factor aspect

Nataf. "To drop, to fall as drops of rain." This Hebrew word occurs 21 times in the Old Testament and four of these times it is used as a term for prophecy. This word reflects the prophetic message as the direct result of divine activity. This Hebrew word was regularly used to describe the falling of rain drops from the heavens (Judges 5:4; Job 36:27; etc.). Yet it is used as a descriptive term for prophecy (Micah 2:6,11).

The prophetic word is also the result of divine activity. It is not only a flow as water from the prophet's lips, gushing forth as a fountain, but it is also to be viewed as rain drops, falling from heaven, the abode of Jehovah. The prophetic word is a word dropped by God from heaven as rain.

New Testament Word

In the New Testament there is only one Greek word, found in five derived forms, which is used to denote "prophecy." There has been much controversy around this word as some scholars have attempted to strip this word of its supernatural element.

Propheteuo. "To prophesy." (Also *prophetes,* "prophet"). This Greek word occurs exactly 200 times in the New Testament in its derived forms. It is a compound word from the Greek verb *phe,* "to say or speak" and the prefix *pro,* meaning either "fore" or "forth" ("fore-telling" or "forth-telling"). It is around this latter Greek prefix that controversy rages among some scholars.

Some insist that the meaning "foretelling" cannot be associated with the word in New Testament times. Kramer, for example, states that the word meant only "speaking forth" and that it didn't obtain the meaning of fore-telling until the second century A.D.[17] Thus the predictive element is thrust out of prophecy, and it is weakened to the level of preaching.

However, it can be conclusively proven that "prophecy" (*propheteuo*) meant "fore-telling" in New Testament times. The Greek preposition *pro* was used in the first century A.D. in both sense of "fore" (called the temporal sense) and "forth" (called the local sense, speaking of positional relationship).[18] It is unquestionably used in the temporal sense of "fore" in Mark 13:11 and 14:8.

It is also found in this sense in numerous papyri and other extrabiblical writings of New Testament times. Indeed, it is found in this sense as early as the Hibeh Papyri, dating from 245 B.C.[19] Also, the early church fathers understood this word in the sense of "fore-telling." As a preposition the local sense of "forth" for *pro* is rare in the New Testament.[20] Therefore, "foretelling" is a well substantiated meaning for the New Testament usage of this word.

Furthermore, it would be expected that this word would carry with it the predictive element of prophecy so familiar in the Old Testament prophetic message. There would be no reason to understand the word losing this sense and every reason to assume that it would retain the connotation from Old Testament concept of prophecy. In the Septuagint, this word, *prophetes,* uniformly translates the Hebrew word for prophet, *nabiy*', a fact which would strongly suggest a close similarity in concept.

The Gospel writers, especially Matthew, seem to emphasize the predictive element in the Old Testament prophets. They frequently make reference to the events of Christ's life as happening in order that it might be fulfilled what was spoken by the Old Testament prophets.

Prophecy and Preaching

There is a tendency on the part of those who reject the supernatural gifts of the Holy Spirit as operative today to define prophecy as preaching. Several modern versions of the New Testament commonly translate prophecy as preaching.

The predictive element in prophecy automatically eliminates prophecy from being fully equated with preaching. Furthermore, there are two different Greek words in the New Testament which are used by the scriptural writers to describe preaching, *euangelizo*, "to preach the Gospel," a comprehensive, broad, and summarizing word, and *kerusso*, "to preach or proclaim." Both of these Greek words are primarily used in the New Testament in the sense of preaching to the lost while New Testament prophecy is clearly directed towards believers (1 Cor. 14:22). These two Greek words for preaching are clearly not used by the scriptural writers as synonyms for prophesy (*propheteuo*).

Some preaching may have a prophetic touch to it. However, prophecy is in the realm of a revealed message proclaimed which is beyond preaching.

The Distinctives of Prophecy

Prophecy may be defined as a declaration of a message from God not known by natural means but by divine revelation, including prediction as well as anointed proclamation. Prophecy then can be distinguished from preaching or any other utterance. The distinctives of prophetic utterances are basically two-fold.

Forth-telling. The distinctive of this form of prophecy is that it necessitates the receiving of a divine revelation before the prophetic proclamation can occur.[21] The prophet speaks for God to the people as the mouthpiece of God. This form includes exhortation, edification, comfort, warning, and even at times judgmental declaration. It speaks to the present situation and often appeals to the past in order to pointedly address the present.

Fore-telling. This form of prophecy is predictive of future events. It may be a proclamation of future blessing or judgment. Often the predictive word is conditional upon the response of the hearers. This predictive element is not an essential part of every prophetic word. A prophecy may be a true and complete prophetic word and function only in a forth-telling aspect. The predictive aspect, however, is a normative function of prophecy in general and would be expected to have a somewhat frequent occurence, especially in a presbytery where seasoned prophets are functioning in the prophetic discourse.

The predictive aspect is vital in prophecy. Since it is the eternal God who speaks through prophets, His words cover the entire span of time, past, present, and future. When eternity becomes involved in the world of time and space, it would be surprising if implications for the future were not present.

Disclosure of the future is ultimately for the benefit of present time. Prediction is not given merely to satisfy man's curiosity about the future. Rather it serves to illuminate what is involved in the needs of the present.

THE NATURE OF PROPHECY

Prophesy in Scripture is more than words spoken in due season. In that the prophet's words are God's words, there comes an inherent authority and power operating with the prophetic word to accomplish it.

The Causative Aspect of Prophecy

In Hebrew thought there was a causal relationship between the prophetic word spoken and the subsequent event following at its own appointed time. The "word" of the Lord was regarded as a living entity, containing within itself divine power to accomplish itself.[22] The spoken prophetic word released a power to perform or to bring about its content.

The creative utterance of God in Genesis, chapter one sets the stage throughout Scripture for the Word of God to possess an intrinsic creative power. The word of the Lord in prophecy is thus a dynamic, creative word.

The prophetic utterance is described in Scripture as being the "word" (Hebrew, *dabar*) of the Lord. So Jeremiah, in 1:9, records God's assurances to him of his prophetic call, "And the Lord said unto me, 'Behold I have put my *words* (Hebrew, *dabar*) in thy mouth.'"

This Hebrew term for "word" (*dabar*) carries with it the connotation of dynamic action. The basic etymological meaning of this term is "to be behind and drive foward" or "to drive forward that which is behind" thus the word (*dabar*) is not only something spoken, but it "drives forward" to accomplish its message. The term developed somehow in Hebrew to portray the function of speaking.

The Hebrew language, especially verbs, have an inherent dynamic character. Hebrew verbs bear a basic meaning always expressing movement or activity, characteristic of the dynamic nature of Hebrew thinking.[23] When a Hebrew verb would express inaction such as a positon of sitting or lying, it would be accomplished by a verb which also designates a movement or action. This is in direct contrast to Greek thinking and language which was by its nature, static and without inherent movement.

This Hebrew term for "word" (*dabar*) meant not only a spoken word but also "deed." The spoken word and its accomplished action were not two different meanings but one basic concept. The speaking of the word was the initial act and the deed accomplished the consequencial act. They were considered two inseparable parts of one process. The accomplishment was inherently an expected event as defined in the very meaning of the term. So Abraham's servant recounted to Isaac all the "things" (Hebrew, *dabar,* "words") he had done (Genesis 24:66), so likewise 1 Kings 11:41 mentions "…the rest of the *acts"* (Hebrew, *dabar,* "words"). Thus in Hebrew the "word" *(dabar)* was identical with action.

In Deuteronomy 18:22, the false prophet is proven to be false in that his words are counterfeit, empty words. They lack the inner power for accomplishing the content of the words:

"When a prophet speaketh in the name of the Lord, if the thing follow not, nor come to pass, that is the thing which the Lord hath not spoken, but the prophet hath spoken it presumptuously: thou shalt not be afraid of him" (Deuteronomy 18:22).

The true prophet, on the other hand, speaks the word of the Lord which drives forward to accomplish its own purpose.

The effective word of prophecy is not alive and invested with a self-realizing power because of the word itself, but rather because it is characteristic of its source, Jehovah Himself. The prophetic word (*dabar*) of the Lord is a manifestation of Jehovah and a revelation of His essence. The living word that issued from God through the mouth of the prophets was never seen as detached from God.

This creative prophetic word is graphically illustrated in Ezekiel 37. As Ezekiel prophesies to the dry bones, they become animate. Ezekiel's prophetic word has all the creative and life-giving power of God's word, because his prophetic word *is* God's word. The prophet's words possess no mysterious or magical powers, but their dynamic nature is because these words are God's words.

The prophetic word which operates today in a presbytery through proven prophets is likewise God's words. Their prophetic utterances as the words of

God initiate a divine process to bring the prophetic message into effect in the lives of those so ministered over in a presbytery. The prophetic word that comes is a creative word.

This is further illustrated by Paul in his first epistle to Timothy:

"Neglect not the gift that is in thee, which was *given thee by prophecy*, with the laying on of the hands of the presbytery" (1 Timothy 4:14).

The gift that Timothy now possessed was given to him "*by* prophecy." This preposition "by" in the Greek is *dia,* meaning literally "through," showing a channel. The prophetic utterance of the presbytery carried with it the creative power that gave (not only just informed) or channeled the gift from God to Timothy. The gift was given to him through the prophetic utterance and its subsequent, effectual work. This verse should also be joined with 2 Timothy 1:6 which shows the gift also being imparted through the laying on of hands as well.

However, a caution must be exercised concerning this truth. One must carefully balance the causal aspect with the conditional aspect of prophecy to avoid taking this truth to an extreme.

THE CONDITIONAL ASPECT OF PROPHECY

Prophecy is conditional. All prophetic messages which come in a presbytery service or in the congregation must be considered as conditional. The creative, effecting power in the prophetic word of God is not automatic nor is it unalterably destined to be fulfilled.

The prophetic word is conditional upon man's response to the word of the Lord. Lack of faith, continuous sin, or a pattern of spiritual instability in a believer's life may either delay or entirely block the fulfillment of God's Word.

God does not overstep human responsibility. Although the prophetic word carries the power to accomplish that word if unhindered, its fulfillment may be hindered by the recipient's life. The prophetic word may thus be never fulfilled.

A graphic example of this is the prophecy of Jonah to Nineveh. His message, "Yet forty days, and Nineveh shall be overthrown" (Jonah 3:4), was expressed in uncompromising terms. Yet the prophecy was obviously conditional, and the prophecy was not fulfilled because of the Ninevite's response.

Some prophetic words in a presbytery will be clearly conditional by the very wording of the message. However, those prophetic utterances which are not expressed in conditional terms must also be considered conditional, for that is God's way of speaking to His people.

Prophecy as a Sign of Blessing

The Apostle Paul made a significant declaration about speaking in tongues and prophecy as both being signs in this age. Paul states in 1 Corinthians 14:21–22 that tongues operate as a sign to unbelievers and prophecy as a sign to believers.

"In the law it is written, 'With men of other tongues and other lips will I speak unto this people; and yet for all that will they not hear me,' saith the Lord. Therefore tongues are for a sign, not to them that believe, but to them that believe not: but prophesying serveth not for them that believe not, but for them which believe" (1 Cor. 14:21–22).

1. In his reference to tongues in verse 22, Paul states that tongues are "for a sign." A sign points to something beyond itself. Trench defines a sign in the New Testament as a miraculous phenomenon pointing to a higher reality beyond itself.[24]

2. Paul refers in verse 22 to tongues being "for a sign." Although the word "sign" isn't repeated regarding prophecy, it is unmistakenly inferred in the original language by Paul that prophecy is "for a sign" to believers as well.[25]

3. This particular expression "*for* a sign" has important significance. This expression in the Greek (*einai eis*) is common in extrabiblical Greek to express the concept of destination.[26] Paul would be using this peculiar Greek construction to convey the idea that each of these two groups, unbelievers and believers, were destined for some special consequence. Tongues and prophecy, by their perpetual operation, continually point as signs to the "higher reality" of the destiny of these respective groups. What is the destiny that each of these two signs signify?

4. Tongues as a sign of judgment. Paul, in these verses, is quoting from Isaiah 28:11–12:

"For with stammering lips and another tongue will he speak to this people, to whom he said, 'This is the rest wherewith ye may cause the weary to rest; and this is the refreshing: yet they would not hear'" (Isaiah 28:11–12).

The reference to another tongue in Isaiah 28:11 was that of the Assyrian tongue as a result of the Assyrian invasion of Judah. The message borne by the Assyrian tongue was not one understood of that tongue but rather a message of God's judgment upon persistent unbelief. God's offer of rest and refreshing was constantly rebuffed, and so God's people must face His judgment. God used the Assyrian conquest and Assyrian tongue to speak of His unwillingness to tolerate continued unbelief.

The use of Isaiah's passage by Paul is quoted to show how the same message is intended to be understood. Paul is showing that just as the Assyrian tongue was a sign of judgment upon His own people because of unbelief, so likewise New Testament tongues function as a sign pointing to the destined judgment to come of all unbelievers if they persist in their unbelief. Every time someone speaks in tongues, whether privately or in the congregation, it is a sign operating that God will yet judge persistent unbelief. Likewise, as long as God tarries in his judgment upon unbelievers, tongues must continue as a warning sign of their destiny.

5. Prophecy as a sign of rest and refreshing. Paul, in his quotation of Isaiah 28:11–12, regarding tongues, omits almost the entirety of verse 12, "To whom he said, This is the rest wherewith ye may cause the weary to rest; and this is the refreshing: *yet they would not hear* (underlined portion only, quoted by Paul in reference to tongues)." However, if God's people would have become "believers" by heeding God's offer to them, they would have had "rest" and "refreshing."

God had offered these blessings repeatedly through the prophetic word. The message drawn by Paul from Isaiah 28:11–12 regarding prophecy is simply that prophecy is a sign to believers that those who exercise belief by heeding the prophetic word inherit the blessings of rest and refreshing.[27]

TONGUES AND PROPHECY AS SIGNS

SIGN	TO WHOM	SIGNIFICANCE
Tongues	Unbelievers	Signifying destiny of judgment for continued unbelief
Prophecy	Believers	Signifying destiny of blessings of rest and refreshing for continued belief and heeding of the word of the Lord

The point here of prophecy as a sign is not only of this blessing coming through the heeding of the prophetic word, but that the continual operation of the prophetic word is also God's sign and promise to us in this age of his progressive blessings upon his believing people. The restoration of presbytery with its prophetic flow is a sign of another visitation of "times of refreshing" (Acts 3:19) and that God will progressively bring His people into rest. Therefore, the prophetic utterance is both a medium as well as God's chosen sign in this age that God will surely fulfill His eternal purposes upon His people of blessing, refreshing, and rest.

THE REALMS OF PROPHECY

Scripture clearly indicates that there are various realms of prophetic flow. Different degrees of unction operate on each of these prophetic levels. Therefore, it is important to have a clear understanding of these varying areas of prophetic function.

The Spirit of Prophecy

This realm of prophetic unction is mentioned in Revelation 19:10, "...the testimony of Jesus is the spirit of prophecy." The spirit of prophecy is the Holy Spirit's mantle of prophetic anointing which is given at various times to a believer (or body of believers) which causes him to prophesy the word of the Lord ("the testimony of Jesus") and without which occasion of special endowment he could not prophesy.

Those who do not have the gift of prophecy and who are not prophets cannot prophesy except when there is a spirit of prophecy upon them. The infrequency of their prophetic flow is rather indicative that they function not by the gift nor in the office but only under the spirit of prophecy.

Moses expressed the wish that all the Lord's people would prophesy (Numbers 11:29). Paul in 1 Corinthians 14:24 and 31 states that all may prophesy. Yet Paul clearly separates this from the office of a prophet and, by contextual implication, the gift of prophecy by the phrasing of his question in 1 Corinthians 12:29, "All are not prophets, are they," requiring a negative answer in the Greek form. Having an anointing on occasions to prophesy is not necessarily indicative of the resident gift of prophecy or the office of a prophet.

When the Holy Spirit moves in a service, a prophetic mantle may at times be upon the congregation, and anyone could prophesy if he exercised faith. This does not happen every service nor is it to be necessarily expected to happen on every occasion of the assembly of God's people.

In Numbers 11:24–30, the seventy elders of Israel all prophesy under the spirit of prophetic anointing. In 1 Samuel 10:10, Saul met a company of prophets, and the Spirit of prophecy likewise came upon Saul and he also prophesied. In 1 Samuel 19:20–24 Saul sent three different groups of messengers, who could not otherwise prophesy, to a company of prophets. The result was that they all prophesied when they came under the spirit of prophecy.

The Gift of Prophecy

The gift of prophecy is mentioned in Romans 12:6 and 1 Corinthians 12:10 as a gift of the Holy Spirit resident within certain believers. Not all have this gift, but it is distributed by the Holy Spirit "severally as he will" (1 Corinthians 12:11).

One who has the gift of prophecy can prophesy on a somewhat regular basis amidst God's people. He need not wait for the special occasions when the Holy Spirit will come upon a congregation with the spirit of prophecy, but rather he can prophesy by reason of his resident gift. The gift of prophecy operates only within the sphere of edification, exhortation, and comfort (1 Corinthians 14:3).

The Office of a Prophet

Ephesians 4:11 declares that the office of a prophet is an ascension gift ministry set in the New Testament church by the Lord. It is a ministry given to the church as a whole. As seen above in the negative question of 1 Corinthians 12:29, not all are prophets even though they may prophesy.

The office of a prophet not only ministers in edification, exhortation, and comfort, but also operates in the realm of guidance, rebuke, judgment, correction, and revelation. The one who has the gift of prophecy but is not a prophet does not function in any of these latter realms.

a. Essentials of the prophetic office

1. An appointed spokesman for God. A basic essential characteristic of the prophetic office is that the prophet is a spokesman for God.

(a) Authority. As an appointed spokesman for God, the prophet's words have the same authority as God's words (see Deut. 18:19). The respect for authority that a true prophet was to receive is inversely implied in the words "you shall not be afraid of him" (i.e., the false prophet; Deuteronomy 18:22). In Genesis 20:7, Abraham is to be reverenced on the grounds of his being a prophet. The Jews carried this respect for the prophetic office even into the times of Christ. Thus the prophetic office brings a realm of spiritual authority into the prophetic ministry not found in the other two realms of prophetic function.

In a presbytery, the authority of the proven prophet should be voluntarily recognized by the host church. Yet the local leadership bears the responsibility of judging the prophet's ministry in prophecy (1 Corinthians 14:29), and the prophet must willingly submit to the ordained authority of the local church. While the prophet's ministry may be a translocal, mobile ministry, his authority is limited to the volition of the local oversight.

(b) Effectual word of prophecy. As a divinely appointed spokesman for God, the prophet's words will have a dynamic and quickening character

to them (see above). So Samuel's reputation as a prophet was confirmed by the fact that "...the Lord was with him and let none of his words fall to the ground (i.e., 'fail')" (1 Samuel 3:19–20).

2. One who is commissioned by God. The Old Testament prophets were launched upon their prophetic careers by a definite call. A prophet had to be commissioned by God or else he was a false prophet. A man could not choose of himself to be a prophet.

- Samuel heard the voice of the Lord in the temple (1 Samuel 3:4–14).
- Elisha was especially chosen by God through Elijah's mantle (1 Kings 19:19).
- Isaiah received a call by a vision of God's glory and the cleansing of his lips (ch. 6).
- Jeremiah was called before birth (1:4), appointed (1:5), and sent (1:7).
- Ezekiel's calling was initiated with "visions" of God (1:1ff).
- Amos, while denying any personal desire for the prophetic ministry, witnesses to his calling (7:14–15).
- Haggai asserts that he was sent by the Lord (1:12).

In the New Testament the call to the prophetic office does not seem to be such a pronounced experience as in Old Testament times. Yet a prophet today must have a definite call to his ministry. In that Christ has given some as prophets to the church (Ephesians 4:11–12), He must have called those particular ones to their prophetic office.

3. A receptor of revelation. A prophet is also a "seer." He must be one who receives revelation, whether visionary, perceptive, or both. Revelation may come through the visionary means of visions and dreams (Numbers 12:6; Hosea 12:10). It may come perceptively through the revelational gifts of the word of knowledge, the word of wisdom, or the discerning of spirits. Every true prophet of God is involved with revelation. Different modes of prophetic revelation will be discussed later.

4. The predictive element. Prediction was a genuine and regular characteristic of the prophetic office.

- Jeremiah indicates that prediction and its fulfillment demonstrated that God had sent a prophet who spoke of peace (Jeremiah 28:9).
- Ezekiel states that the fulfillment of his words would be the proof that a prophet had been in their midst (Ezekiel 33:32–33).
- Peter states that the prophets predicted the grace to come (1 Peter 1:10).
- The Gospels repeatedly relate the life of Christ as the fulfillment of the prophet's predictions.
- The New Testament prophet Agabus predicted a famine and the imprisonment of Paul (Acts 11:27–28; 21:10–11).
- Luke indicated that all of the prophets participated in predictive aspects regarding the events of Christ's first coming (Acts 3:18) and events surrounding Christ's second coming (Acts 3:21,20).

  Acts 3:24, "Yea, and all the prophets from Samuel and those that follow after, as many as have spoken, have likewise foretold of these days."

  Therefore, if all of the prophets participated in the predictive element of prophecy, it must be regarded as an essential of the prophetic office.

However, prediction is not part of every prophetic message. With certain prophets, prediction may be prominent while with others it is more an exception. Yet prediction is a part of their prophetic office.

Inscripturation

The fourth realm of prophetic function is that of inscripturation. Inscripturated revelation is "new" revelation which becomes authoritative as Scripture. This is obviously the highest level of prophetic revelation. This level of revelation is "inspiration" (2 Timothy 3:16, Gk., *theopneustos,* "God-breathed"), and as such demands a place alongside of the rest of God's written Word. It is inerrant and infallible.

Inscripturated revelation is not being given today. God is no longer adding to His written Word, nor does He give new revelation today (Revelation 22:18–19). This may be seen from the following reasons:

a. Not all prophetic messages are inscripturated revelation

Several biblical examples will suffice to show this fact.

- The messages of the seventy elders who prophesied were not recorded as Scripture (Numbers 11:24–30).
- The message of Saul's prophecy was not retained in Scripture for succeeding generations (1 Samuel 10:10–11; 19:18–24).
- Many of the prophetic songs of David's "singing prophets" (1 Chronicles 25:1–8) were not included in the Psalter as Scripture.
- Many of the prophetic words of Judas and Silas (Acts 15:32) as well as Agabus are not recorded in Scripture.

b. The progressive principle

Divine revelation was unfolded in time progressively. New revelation did not complete itself in one exhaustive act but unfolded itself in a long series of acts, followed by further revelation. Word-revelation followed act-revelation. Significant events in God's time scale gave rise to further word-revelation, which through the prophets divinely interpreted these events to the people. Each new revelation, however, further enlarged upon prior revelation.

Therefore, even the messages of the Old Testament prophets were built upon and consistent with God's prior revelation in history. This was so because of the nature of God and also the nature of prophecy. God's revelation to men through the prophets must be consistent with itself, and its revelational character must be based on prior revelation, rather than fragmented and disjointed.

c. The covenant relationship of Old Testament prophecy

The message of the prophets consisted of illuminative revelation (interwoven with prediction) from God regarding Israel's relationship to God and His covenant with Israel. God gave them divine prophetic interpretation of the covenant for their times.

- The prophetic message is clearly related to the law. In 2 Kings 17:13 the people were told to "keep My statues according to all the law which I commanded your fathers, and which I sent to you through my servants the prophets."

- The prophets are shown to be continually sent to warn of covenant violations and to call the people to repent (2 Chronicles 6:14–16).[28]
- Elijah showed by his choice of Horeb that he united his work to that of Moses and the covenant (1 Kings 19:9–18).
- The prophets Isaiah and Micah also based some of their prophetic messages upon the prior revelation of the Davidic Covenant.
- The prophet was to be regarded as a man of the Word already revealed. Jeremiah 18:18, "…for the law shall not perish from the priest, nor counsel from the wise, nor the word from the prophet…."
- Even the prophetic work of Christ is based upon God's prior revelation. Matthew 5:17, "Think not that I am come to destroy the law, or the prophets: I am not come to destroy, but to fulfill."

d. Christ as the climax of all revelation

The writer of Hebrews shows us that Christ is the culmination of new revelation. In the manner that God spoke by inspiration to the Old Testament prophets, so now in these last days this process of inscripturated revelation reaches its progressive climax in the prophetic ministry of Christ.[29]

Hebrews 1:1–2, "God who at sundry time and in divers manners spake in time past unto the fathers by the prophets, hath in these last days spoken unto us by his *Son,* whom he hath appointed heir of all things, by whom also he made the worlds."

Thus the New Testament scriptures are called "the law of Christ" (Galatians 6:2).

Therefore, any other new revelation would be anticlimactic in God's program. There is also no need for further "new" revelation from prophets today.

In Paul's writings the Greek word for "revelation," *apokalupsis*, is used primarily of the eschatological appearance of the Lord Jesus Christ and its associated events (Romans 2:5; 8:19; 1 Corinthians 1:7). Any further "new" revelation awaits the second coming of Christ whose coming itself will be a "revelation."

e. *The limitation of New Testament prophecy*

There is a direct limitation put upon all New Testament prophecy. Paul, in 1 Corinthians, restricted such prophecy in this age to that which is based upon prior revelation.

1 Corinthians 13:9, 12, "For we know in part, and we prophesy in part.... For now we see through a glass, darkly; but then face to face: now I know in part; but then shall I know even as also I am known."

Verse 12 shows that partial knowledge is continual in this age until we are "face to face" with Christ at His second coming. Full knowledge, as against this partial knowledge, is defined in verse 12 as absolute knowledge as God has knowledge of us personally. This is a claim to access of God's omniscience. At the second coming of Christ, man will exercise knowledge to the same degree as God exercises knowledge of man. This tapping of the divine attribute could only be possible when Christ returns.

The accessibility of what we can know now in partial knowledge is limited to what God has given us in His written word. Through God's written Word, "we know in part" (vs. 9).

Prophecy likewise has this same limitation put upon it. New Testament prophecy can only operate "in part," according to the portion of knowledge granted us now in the prior revelation of God's written word. Therefore, no "new" revelation could come which is not already given in the "part" made known to us in the written Word. Yet the prophetic function of the New Testament prophet continues (Ephesians 4:11–13), parallel to and illuminating that which we "know in part."

Moses received "new" revelation directly or "face to face" (Numbers 12:6–8). Christ also held this same privilege with the father[30] and was a prophet like unto Moses (Deuteronomy 18:15,18). After Moses, no prophet, except Christ, had such a relationship in revelation. Thus the latter prophets, though inspired with inscripturated revelation, had their revelations granted by God based upon prior revelation through Moses and later revelations.

Deuteronomy 34:10, "And there arose not a prophet since in Israel like unto Moses, whom the Lord new face to face."

First Corinthians 13:12 shows that one day we likewise will be "face to face" with God to know all revelation, but now revelation is limited. Therefore, revelation is limited to God's prior revelation of His written Word. The Prophetic word must then be judged by the written Word (1 Corinthians 14:29).

f. Present revelation

Two realms of present revelation may be received today. These are the following realms:

1. Illuminative revelation. This realm of revelation would be that which illumines or enlightens particularly the propositional truth already given in God's written Word. Also it may be that revelation which is based on the principles of God's written Word which are directed prophetically to special needs or situations within the lives of those receiving this word. The Greek word for "revelation," *apokalupsis*, is used in this sense of illumination in Ephesians 1:17 and Philippians 3:15.

2. Informational revelation. This realm of revelation is that which is made known to the prophet of specific information regarding people's lives, needs, problems, or sins. It includes the special revelation of prediction. Agabus is a good example of such revelation (Acts 11:27–28; 21:10–11).

This revelation is received either through the visionary modes or the revelational gifts of the Holy Spirit (see below). This realm includes the function of prophetic revelation as envisioned by Paul in his great chapter on prophecy, 1 Corinthians 14. 1 Corinthians 14:25, "And thus are the secrets of his heart made manifest; and so falling down on his face he will worship God, and report that God is in you of a truth."

This specific information received in revelation is always consistent with God's prior revelation, although not necessarily containing the content of Scripture.

Caution must be exercised in this realm of revelation. Only mature and proven prophetic ministries should attempt to function freely in this area of revelation. If someone believes he is receiving informational revelation at times, he should share it first privately with his local church leadership and let it be judged before it is given publically or shared with anyone else. Even when genuine, informational revelation is received, wisdom does not always dictate a public declaration of this revelation even among mature prophetic ministries.

In a presbytery, both illuminative and informational revelation will be operative. By this manner God both speaks in principles and practically probes deep into the lives of the candidates that they may profit and grow in God.

Realm of Revelation	Time Span	Nature of Revelation
Illuminative Revelation	Operative today	Enlightens principles based upon God's written Word and applies them prophetically to people's situations
Informational Revelation	Operative today	Specific information about people's lives and situations
Inscripturated Revelation	NOT operative today	New revelation received by inspiration of the Spirit, to be as authoritative and equated with God's written revelation

MODE OF PROPHETIC REVELATION

A study of the mode of prophetic revelation involves a look at two essential aspects of revelation. The mode of receiving revelation from God and the mode of delivery of this revelation from God must be considered.

The Mode of Receiving Prophetic Revelation

There were four modes of revelation used by God in making known His mind to His prophets. A study of these modes will indicate the supernatural character of the revelation.

Verbal Revelation

The most prominent means of revelation is that of the spoken word. The prophets mention in hundreds of instances of Scripture, "Thus saith the Lord." Thus they witness to God's verbal revelation to them of that which they prophesy to others.

a. Vocal revelation

There are numerous Scriptural instances in which God spoke in an audible voice. God used actual words to communicate a vocal message to man. Several examples will illustrate this means.

- At Mount Sinai, God spoke audibly to Moses so that the people could also hear His voice (Exodus 19:9).
- The voice of the Lord spoke audibly to Samuel so as to be mistaken for Eli's voice (1 Samuel 3:1–14).
- God's voice was heard from heaven at the water baptism of Christ (Matthew 3:17).
- God spoke audibly at the occasion of Christ's transfiguration (Matthew 17:5).
- God's voice confirmed audibly the prayer of Jesus regarding His glorification (John 12:28).
- Saul of Tarsus heard the audible voice of the Lord on the road to Damascus (Acts 9:4–6).

It is possible for God to speak audibly today, but this is infrequent and rather unusual. Such rare occasion of vocal revelation would be mostly informational revelation. One should not seek, plead with God, nor expect this means of God's communication. No amount of prayer and fasting can earn this form of revelatory visitation.

b. Non-vocal revelation

Most verbal revelation was non-vocal in nature. God spoke directly to the heart of the prophets without audible sounds. The prophet received this divine message in accurate terms. The message was spoken by God in the inner spirit of the prophet, received by Him through a direct, divine impression. This mode of revelation will occur most frequently today.

Visionary Revelation

Visionary revelation is manifested in three different ways.

1. Dreams. Dreams were considered a valid way for a prophet to receive a message from God.

Numbers 12:6, "If there be a prophet among you, I the Lord will make myself known unto him in a vision, and will speak unto him in a dream."

- God spoke in a dream to Abraham (Genesis 15:12–17), who was a patriarchal prophet (Genesis 20:7).
- God spoke through dreams to Jacob (Genesis 28:12; 31:10), who was also declared to be a patriarchal prophet (Psalms 105:15).
- God spoke likewise in a dream to the Prophet Daniel, chapter 7.

However, dreams as divine communications from God were not limited to the prophets.

(a) The heathen received dreams from God:

Abimelech (Genesis 20:3); Laban (Genesis 31:24); the Midianite (Judges 7:13–14); Pharaoh's butler and baker (Genesis 40:5); Pharaoh (Genesis 41:7, 15–26); Nebuchadnezzar (Daniel 2:1,4,36); the three wise men (Matthew 2:12); Pilate's wife (Matthew 27:19).

(b) God's people who were not prophets received dreams from God:

Joseph (Genesis 37:5,9,10,20); Solomon (1 Kings 3:5); Joseph (Matthew 1:20).

Dreams as a divine mode of revelation are promised in this age. Joel 2:28, "And it shall come to pass afterward, that I will pour out my spirit upon all flesh...your old men shall dream dreams...."

2. Visions. Visions are closely associated with dreams, the vision occurring, however, during a time when the individual is fully awake and conscious. Unlike dreams, visions are distincively characteristic of the office of a prophet. The term "seer" as applied to a prophet referred to his seeing visions (Numbers 12:6). Visions may be seen by the prophet in the following manner:

- External vision—optical perception.

An example of this means was that of Elisha who visually saw the supernatural host of God encompassing the city of Dothan and prayed to Jehovah that his servant also might see this sight (2 Kings 6:17).

- Internal vision—inner perception.

Zechariah's night visions were most likely perceived in this fashion, as the prophet was "awakened" in preparation for the visions (Zechariah 1–6; cf. 4:1). Many of the prophet's visions cannot be easily categorized, however, as to which manner of visionary perception they were.

The prophets varied in degree of visionary revelation. In Daniel, Ezekiel, and Zechariah, the visionary mode is most prominent. No biblical writer equals Daniel in *visions* with the exception of John *in* the book of Revelation. While *visions* are the exception in some prophets, it is the rule in Daniel.[31] In Jeremiah, visions seem to be more frequent than in Isaiah.

Visions of the Canonical Prophets:

- *Isaiah.* Vision of the Lord and His glory (ch. 6); valley of vision (ch. 22).
- *Jeremiah.* An almond rod (1:11); a seething pot (1:13); two baskets of figs (24:1–2).
- *Ezekiel.* Vision of the glory of God (1:3, 12–14; 23); vision of the roll (2:9); vision of the man of fire (eh. 8–9); vision of the coals of fire (10:1–7); vision of dry bones (37:1–14);

vision of Jerusalem and the temple (Ch. 4-0–18); vision of the waters (47:1–12).

- *Daniel.* A secret vision (2:19); vision of the four beasts (7:1–8); vision of the Ancient of Days (7:9–27); vision of the ram and the goat (8:1–14); vision of the angel (Ch. 10); vision of world powers (11:2–12:4); vision of the man clothed in linen (12:5–13).
- *Amos.* Vision of grasshoppers (7:1–2); vision of fire (7:4); vision of a plumbline (7:7–8); vision of summer fruit (8:1–2); vision of the temple (9:1–3).
- *Zechariah.* Vision of horses (1:8–11); vision of horns and carpenters (1:18–21); vision of the high priest (3:1–5); vision of the golden candlestick (Ch. 4); vision of the flying roll (5:1–4); vision of the mountains and chariots (6:1–8).

No visions occur in the books of the prophets Hosea, Joel, Obadiah, Jonah, Micah, Nahum, Habakkuk, Zephaniah, Haggai, and Malachi. Visions were seen in New Testament times by Zacharias (Luke 1:11–17), Stephen (Acts 7:55–56), Paul (Acts 9:3–5,12; 16:9; 18:9–10; 2 Corinthians 12:1–4), Ananias (Acts 9:10–12), Cornelius (Acts 10:3), Peter (Acts 10:9–18), and John (Book of Revelation). Visions were also promised to continue in this age by Joel (2:28).

In a presbytery, visionary revelation may be received by a prophet. Its meaning may or may not be fully understood by the prophet receiving the vision. He will usually describe the vision and give what explanation to it that he does perceive. As with the canonical prophets of Scripture, some prophets today have a stronger visionary prophetic ministry while others are more verbal revelatory prophets. Neither is exclusive of the other, nor does the prominence of one mode make that prophet necessarily greater than another prophet.

3. Trances. A trance is a visional state in which revelation is received. This rapturous state is one in which a prophet would perceptively be no longer limited to natural consciousness and volition. He is "in the Spirit" where full consciousness of the natural may be temporarily transcended.[32]

A clear example of this state is that of the Apostle Paul who was in the Spirit caught up to the third heaven (2 Corinthians 12:1–4). He states that his state of trance was such that he was unable to discern whether he was out of the body or in it (12:2).

The Greek word for "trance" is *ekstasis*, from which we get the word ecstacy, found in Acts 10:10; 11:5; 22:17. A trance, however, is not an ecstatic state in which the prophet is in some wild state or mentally or emotionally out of control of himself.

1 Corinthians 14:32, "And the spirits of the prophets are subject to the prophets."

There are scriptural references which mention the prophets as madmen (2 Kings 9:11; Jeremiah 29:26), or fools (Hosea 9:7). However, a closer study will show that these designations are the contentions of the prophets' critics who assert this of them in mockery.

Scriptural Examples of Trances:

- Abraham. A state of deep sleep prepared Abraham for God's revelation to him (Genesis 15:12).
- Ezekiel. Ezekiel was lifted up in the Spirit and transported away to Telabib by the river Chebar (Ezekiel 3:14–15), to Jerusalem (8:3), and to Chaldea (11:24).
- Daniel. Daniel in prophetic rapture fell to the ground and went into a deep sleep (8:15–18; see also 10:7–10).
- Peter. Peter fell into a trance accompanied by a vision (Acts 10:10–15; 11:5).
- Paul. Paul likewise was in a trance and saw a vision of the Lord in the temple (Acts 22:17–21) and Paradise (2 Corinthians 12:1–4).

The Mode of Delivering Prophetic Revelation

The prophets received revelation from God in order that they would deliver their messages to the people as they had received them. There was great diversity, however, in the manner of their delivery of this revelation.

The writer of Hebrews stated of the prophets:

Hebrews 1:1, "God, who at sundry times and in divers manners spake in time past unto the fathers by the prophets."

The phrase "at sundry times and in divers manners" was written in the Greek, p*olumeros kai polutropos,* a familiar literary form of Greek alliteration.[33] It literally means, "in many parts and in many ways." Each prophet contributed various parts of prophetic revelation, and this was done in many varied ways. These many ways can be basically summarized under three categorical ways in which the prophets conveyed their messages.

Revelation through the Prophets' Words

Prophetic revelation was most often delivered through the verbal model of delivery.

a. Spoken word

Prophetic revelation might be delivered in a spoken word as seen in Elijah's prophecy to Ahab (1 Kings 17:1ff) or Nathan's prophecy to David (2 Samuel 12), and many others.

b. Written word

The prophetic message might be also delivered through the written Word as seen in the books of Isaiah, Jeremiah, and Daniel. The majority of the prophets' revelations differed greatly in style of expression, emphasis, and intensity. Their words were often highly figurative and poetic.

c. The language of the prophets

The prophets' language included the following kinds of speech: riddles, parables, allegory, metaphors, similes, hyperboles, personifications, and others.

One of the most outstanding characteristics of prophetic delivery is symbolism. Daniel is probably the most graphic Old Testament example. Daniel carefully shows that the symbols he uses are to be understood as symbols by the explanations that accompany them.[34] The most graphic example of symbolism in the New Testament is the book of Revelation, containing approximately 350 symbols, the meaning of which may be unlocked when traced back to their Old Testament usage.

In a presbytery, the prophetic word may at times come forth from the prophets in similar language of parables, metaphors, similes, or the like. This prophetic language serves to convey more clearly in pictorial imagery what God is saying to the candidates. Other times the prophetic word will be plain and direct.

d. The prophetic perfect

The Hebrew language of the Old Testament has only two tenses, the perfect and the imperfect. These two tenses do not entirely parallel our English tenses, which regard tense in the sense of time. The Hebrew people rather considered the completion or incompletion of the action as important. The perfect tense indicated that the action was completed while the imperfect indicated that the action was still to be completed.

There was an unique peculiarity about the prophet's language. When the prophets prophesied about some future event, they would often use the tense of completed action, the perfect tense. The prophet thus was stating a predictive word as an already accomplished event. This procedure was the result of the spirit of faith of the prophet, who was so certain of the fulfilment of his word that he stated it as an already accomplished event.

One of the best known examples is that of Isaiah 9:6 when the future birth of Christ is predicted, "For unto us a child is born...." In the Hebrew, the prophetic perfect literally reads, "a child *has been born*." Yet this event would not be fulfilled for over seven centuries.

Revelation through the Prophet's Life

Revelation was conveyed not only by words but also by the life of the prophet.

Hosea. Hosea was married to a harlot to symbolize the spiritual adultery of unfaithful Israel (Hosea 1–3). The life experience of Hosea symbolized Israel's apostasy. Thus Hosea lived out the prophetic message of the tender love and forgiving compassion of Jehovah towards Israel. Hosea's life with Gomer was a prophetic parable in history of the Lord who would one day save His unfaithful wife by purchasing her from slavery, shame, and sin (Hosea 3:1–2).

Jonah. The book of Jonah is one of the books of the Minor Prophets. Yet it contains only one prophecy in the book (Jonah 3:4), and that prophecy was not fulfilled (because of the conditional aspect of the prophecy). How is it then prophetic? Jonah's life was a prophetic message to Israel of future events.

- Chapter one. Jonah's failure to be a witness to the Gentiles (Nineveh) caused him to be judged of God. This prophetically portrays Israel's failure to be a witness to the Gentiles and her subsequent judgment.
- Chapter two. Jonah's imprisonment in a great fish for three days and three nights and his subsequent deliverance pictured the death and resurrection of Christ. Christ verified this as prophetic of Himself (Matthew 12:40).
- Chapter three. The name "Jonah" means "dove" in the Hebrew language. Chapter three pictures through Jonah this present age, the age of God's Dove, the Holy Spirit, with God's Word being taken to the Gentiles and a great harvest of souls repenting.
- Chapter four. Here Jonah pictures the church of the end time, sitting in his tabernacle ("booth," Hebrew, *succah,* meaning "tabernacle") and having his character and attitudes changed by God in a time of severe tribulation.

Naming of prophets' children. Some prophets were commanded by God to give symbolical names to their own offspring. Thus the children's entire lives also served as a prophetic message to Israel.

- *Isaiah.* Isaiah named one son Shear Jashub, meaning "a remnant shall return" (Isaiah 7:3). This name conveyed in the son's life a prophetic promise; Isaiah named another son *Maher-shalal-hash-baz,* meaning "the spoil speedeth, the prey hasteth," which prophetically promised judgment (8:1).[35]
- *Hosea.* Hosea named his eldest son Jezreel (1:4), meaning "sowing, or scattering." This name had a double prophetic intent,

promising scattering for Israel (Isaiah 1) but the sowing for spiritual Israel (2:23); Hosea named his daughter Lo-ruhamah, meaning "no mercy," a judgment upon Israel (1:6); The prophet named his second son Lo-ammi, meaning "not my people," indicating God's rejection of Israel (1:9).

Revelation through the Prophets' Actions

The symbolical acts of the prophets were also vehicles for delivering divine revelation. The prophetic act was itself as much a mode of divine revelation as was the prophet's words. The symbolical act was a graphic means of gaining the attention of the people, and dramatizing God's message to them.

Symbolical Acts of the Prophets

a. Isaiah. Isaiah walked naked and barefoot to symbolize the similar fate awaiting Egypt and Ethiopia from Assyria (Isaiah 20:1–6).

b. Jeremiah. Jeremiah walked through the streets, wearing a yoke around his neck to signify future Babylonian bondage Jeremiah, chapters 27–28).

c. Ezekiel.

- Ezekiel was commanded to portray upon tile a mock attack of Jerusalem (Ezekiel 4:1–3).
- Ezekiel was commanded to lie upon his left side for 390 days and 40 days on his right side (4:4–8).
- He was commanded to eat different kinds of unclean food, for 390 days, depicting Israel's lack in exile (4:9–17).
- He was told to burn a third part of his hair, symbolizing the future destruction of Jerusalem (5:1–4).
- Ezekiel was exhorted to prophesy to dry bones (Chapter 37).

d. The Prophet Ahijah. Ahijah tore Jeroboam's garment into twelve pieces, thus symbolizing the dividing of the kingdom (1 Kings 11:30ff).

e. Agabus. Agabus bound his own hands and feet with Paul's girdle, thus depicting the future binding of Paul at Jerusalem (Acts 21:11). These are only a portion of the symbolic acts of the prophets.

Symbolical acts of prophets could happen today. However, such acts would be more the exception and not the norm. In a presbytery prophetic revelation will mostly come through the mode of prophetic words, not acts.

THE SOURCES OF PROPHETIC REVELATION

The Scriptures teach that a prophetic word could possibly come from any one of three sources. These sources are the following:

The Holy Spirit

The Holy Spirit is the only source of a true prophetic word. 2 Peter 1:21, "For the prophecy came not in old time by the will of man: but holy men of God spake as they were *moved* by the Holy Spirit."

The Holy Spirit "moved" these prophets. The Greek word for "moved," *phero*, means "to be borne along" or even "driven along as by a wind" (cf. Acts 27:15–17). The Holy Spirit, as the wind and breath of God, "bore along" the prophets as a direct source of their revelation.

The Human Spirit

(Ezekiel 13:1–6; Jeremiah 23:16). This is one who is speaking out of his own heart. His prophetic words are not the revelation of God, but are his imaginations coming from his own spirit. Ezekiel 13:1–2, "...that prophesy out of their own hearts...Woe unto the foolish prophets, that follow their own spirit, and have seen nothing."

The Evil Spirit

The source in this instance is a satanic lying spirit. This spirit is evident in false prophets, but not necessarily restricted to them.

A prophecy can even be a mixture of any of these sources. This is possible, because men as prophetic mouthpieces are yet in an imperfect state. No prophetic ministry, except Christ, was ever a perfect channel.

A graphic example of this mixture is the Apostle Peter who had just received the revelation, "Thou art the Christ, the Son of the living God"

(Matthew 16:16). Jesus confirmed that this revelation had its source in God, "flesh and blood hath not revealed it unto thee, but my Father which is in heaven" (vs. 17).

Only minutes later Jesus had to rebuke Peter who had just stated a prophetic revelation in the predictive realm, saying that the death and subsequent resurrection of Christ as foretold by Him would not occur (vs. 22). Jesus recognized the source of this prophetic word as satanic and rebuked Satan as speaking through Peter's lips.

Matthew 16:23, "But He turned, and said unto Peter, 'Get thee behind me, Satan: thou art an offence unto me: for thou savourest not the things that be of God, but those that be of men.'"

Does this mean that we fear prophecy or that prophecy is unsafe? No, we are not to despise prophecy. 1 Thessalonians 5:20, "Despise not prophesyings."

It does mean, however, that personal prophecy should only come from those who are mature and proven ministries. Mature ministries have learned to know the voice of God and to be sensitive of the source of their prophetic revelation. Younger and immature ministries who attempt to move in this sphere can cause havoc in people's lives.

It also requires that a prophetic word must be judged. The judging of prophecy provides a safeguard for the people against a word which would contain mixture.

Judging the Prophetic Word

Prophecy is Not a Perfect Gift

As seen above, inscripturated revelation was perfect and inerrant. However, a prophetic revelation today does not operate on this sphere of inspiration. Thus there is always the possibility of mixture in the prophetic word.

The fact that prophecy is open for judgment in this age proves its present, imperfect state. The imperfect state of prophecy is because of the imperfect state of the channels through which it comes (1 Corinthians 14:29).

Proving the Prophetic Word

The basis of testing the prophetic source of any prophecy is eight-fold. The prophetic word may be proven by the following means.

Content of the prophetic word

Paul clearly stated that prophecy is to be proven on the basis of its content. He indicated that at times there will be content which is not good. The good of the prophetic word is to be held fast, and that which is not good should be rejected.

1 Thessalonians 5:20–21, "Despise not prophesyings. Prove all things; hold fast that which is good."

The content of the prophetic word may be proven in the following ways:

- *The Criterion of the Written Word.* The prophetic word is tested on the basis of whether it conforms in content with the principles and precepts of the written Word of God. Does it line up with the testimony of Jesus? Thus, Revelation 19:10 states, "the testimony of Jesus is the spirit of prophecy."

- *A Comparison of the Written Word.* Does the prophetic word speak according to the whole of Scripture? Isaiah 8:19–20, "should not a people seek unto their God?...To the law and to the testimony: if they speak not according to this word, it is because there is no light in them."

- *The Commandments of the Written Word.* Does the prophetic word exhort and command in accordance with the specific commandments of God's written Word? Deuteronomy 13:1–4, "If there arise among you a prophet, or a dreamer of dreams...saying, 'Let us go after other gods, which thou hast not known, and let us serve them,' thou shalt not hearken unto the words of that prophet, or that dreamer of dreams; for the Lord your God proveth you.... Ye shall walk after the Lord your God, and fear him, and keep his commandments, and obey his voice...."

- *The Character of the Prophetic Word.* The spirit in which the prophetic word is given also proves the word. The Holy Spirit never speaks in terms of condemnation. The Spirit may bring a true word of rebuke or even judgment, yet it comes forth in a spirit of tenderness. It purposes to bring restoration and to lift up the individual. A word of a harsh tone which would leave the hearer devastated, depressed, and condemned is not from God. Romans 8:1, "There is therefore now no condemnation to them which are in Christ Jesus...." (cf. Romans 8:34).

- *The Consequence of Fulfilment.* Especially in the predictive realm, the matter of fulfilment in times proves a prophetic word. Deuteronomy 18:22, "When a prophet speaketh in the name of the Lord, if the thing follow not, nor come to pass, that is the thing which the Lord hath not spoken, but the prophet hath spoken it presumptuously...."

- *The Conduct of the Prophets.* Scripture teaches that the life-style of a prophet who is not righteous automatically makes his prophetic words suspect.

Jeremiah 23:15–16, "For from the prophets of Jerusalem is profaneness gone forth into all the land. Thus saith the Lord of hosts, 'Hearken not unto the words of the prophets that prophesy unto you; they make you vain; they speak a vision of their own heart, and not out of the mouth of the Lord.'"

Therefore, we are to try the spirits of those who claim to be prophets.

1 John 4:1, "Beloved, believe not every spirit, but try the spirits whether they are of God: because many false prophets are gone out into the world."

A presbytery must utilize apostles and prophets who not only have proven ministries but also proven lives.

- *The Confirmation of the Spirit.* Another means of testing a prophetic word is whether the word bears witness with our inner spirit through the Holy Spirit resident within us. Romans 8:16, "The Spirit beareth witness with our spirit...." (cf. 1 John 2:20, 27). This is, however, the most subjective of all the ways of proving a prophetic word and likewise the most unreliable. Therefore, caution should be exercised against indiscriminate accepting or rejecting of prophetic words on this basis alone. This means of proving a prophetic word should be coupled with one of the other ways of testing a word. Local church leadership must make the final judgment call on these matters.

• *The Confirmation of Other Witnesses.* The law of confirmation must be applied to the proving of prophetic words which involve important decisions and significant changes in direction. 2 Corinthians 13:1, "In the mouth of two or three witnesses shall every word be established."

Any such word should be proven by the confirmation of others. Since much of the prophetic flow in a presbytery is a word of confirmation, the needed witness to a former prophetic word of the revealed will of God often comes at this time.

If such a significant word comes for the first time to a candidate in a presbytery without other confirmation, he should wait for a later confirmation of this word. This does not mean that he rejects the word nor even suspects it. He can even tentatively accept it as from the Lord, yet he waits for a confirmation before moving in the areas mentioned in the word. He holds the prophetic word until the confirmation comes.

God is always ready to confirm His word. If it is a true prophetic word, it will be confirmed. The candidate must exercise patience until confirmation comes. If confirmation does not come in time, then the original word should not be accepted.

The Responsibility of Judging Prophecy

The prophetic word should be judged by those who are established leadership. Those who are not leadership should not presume to make this judgment alone, but trust those who are prophets and have mature oversight to determine this matter. The leadership, however, must not default in this area of responsibility.

1 Corinthians 14:29, "Let the prophets speak two or three, and let the others judge."

When a prophetic word is negatively judged, it should be handled in a spirit of love. If the prophetic word has been given publically, often a brief statement will suffice to inform the people that this word has been judged by the leadership as not from God. Judging or correcting a bad word should be done, if possible, in the service when it occurs. Much wisdom and tact is needed in handling such a matter.

DESCRIPTIONS OF THE PROPHETS

DEVELOPMENT OF THE PROPHETIC OFFICE

The Development of False Prophets

False prophets were in abundance in the heathen nations surrounding God's people. Their mediums of revelation were divination and other occult practices (Deuteronomy 18:1–14).

The development of false prophets, while influenced by the heathen false prophets (Deuteronomy 13:1–2; Zechariah 13:2), had its greatest impetus in the time of the monarchy. Apostasy came in the kings of Israel and Judah. True prophets denounced the wicked kings while these kings viewed the true prophets with suspicion and antagonism. False prophets arose who found it more convenient to be loyal to a corrupt king but disloyal to God. They prophesied for advantage and personal gain (Micah 3:5–11).

The Development of True Prophets

Scripture clearly suggests that the prophetic office has operated from the time of creation:

Acts 3:21, "...which God hath spoken by the mouth of all his holy *prophets since the world began.*"

Luke 11:50–51, "That the blood of all the prophets, which was shed from the foundation of the world, may be required of this generation; from the blood of Abel unto the blood of Zacharias...."

Here, Luke indicates that Abel was a prophet. Jeremiah spoke of prophets who were from ancient times (Jeremiah 28:8; cf. 7:13,25). The Gospel writers repeatedly make references to "the prophets of old" (Matthew 5:12; 11:13: 14:5; 16:14; 23:30; Mark 6:15; Luke 1:70; 6:23).

a. *The Pre-Mosaic Prophets* *(4000–1450 B.C.)*

- Pre-Patriarchal Prophets. The prophets before Moses which are identified for us as such are the following:
  - Abel (Luke 11:50–51).
  - Enoch (Jude 14) who prophesied regarding the second coming of the Lord with ten thousands of his saints.
  - Noah who prophesied concerning the flood and his own descendants (Hebrews 11:7; 1 Peter 3:20; Genesis 9:25–27).

- Patriarchal Prophets.
  - Abraham (Genesis 20:7; Psalms 105:9–15).
  - Isaac foretold future events (Psalms 105:9–15; Hebrews 11:20).
  - Jacob (Psalms 105:9–15; Genesis 48:13–49:27) who prophesied over Joseph's son and his own sons.
  - Joseph (Psalms 105:15–23; Genesis 50:24; Hebrews 11:22) who prophesied regarding the future exodus from Egypt.

b. *Prophets of the Mosaic Period* *(1450–1050 B.C.)*

- Moses, who was the first great Hebrew prophet (Deuteronomy 34:10).
- Miriam, a prophetess (Exodus 15:20).
- Aaron (Exodus 7:1).
- Deborah, a prophetess (Judges 4:4).
- An anonymous prophet (Judges 6:8).
- Hannah, possibly a prophetess (1 Samuel 2:1–10).

c. *Prophets of the early Monarchy Period* *(1050–931 B.C.)*

The prophetic plea here was mainly national. The prophets spoke of repentance and conversion.

- Samuel (1 Samuel; Acts 3:24).
- Nathan (2 Samuel 7:2–17; 12:1–22; 1 Kings 1:8–4.5).
- Gad (1 Samuel 22:5; 1 Chronicles 21:9–19).
- David (Acts 1:16; 2:30; 4:25; Hebrews 11:32).

d. *Prophets of the divided Monarchy Period* *(931–845 B.C.)*

- Ahijah prophesied the division of the kingdom (1 Kings 11).
- Shemaiah who prophesied to Rehoboam (1 Kings 12).
- Iddo who saw visions against Jeroboam (2 Chronicles 9:29).
- Jehaziel (2 Chronicles 20:14–24).
- Eliezer (2 Chronicles 20:37).
- Two anonymous prophets who prophesied judgment to Jeroboam's house (1 Kings 13).
- The prophet Jehu who prophesied against Baasha, king of Israel (1 Kings 16:1–7).
- Hanani, who prophesied a rebuke to Asa, king of Judah (2 Chronicles 16:7).
- Zechariah, son of Jehoiada the priest, who was slain for his prophetic utterances (2 Chronicles 24:20–21; Luke 11:49–51).
- Micaiah who denounced Ahab (1 Kings 22).
- Elijah prophesied during the time of King Ahab and Jezebel (1 Kings 17–2 Kings 1).
- Elisha, last of the pre-canonical prophets (2 Kings 2–13).
- School of the Prophets, which overlapped into the time of the canonical prophets (1 Samuel 10:5).

e. *Prophets of the Canonical Period* *(845–400 B.C.)*

These prophets prophesied of repentance for the divided kingdom. Here they developed an apocalyptic thrust and the revelation of the future church. Their books contain their prophecies.

- Pre-exilic Prophets:
  Obadiah, Joel, Jonah, Amos, Hosea, Micah, Isaiah, Jeremiah, Nahum, Zephaniah, Habakkuk.

- Exilic Prophets:
  Ezekiel, Daniel.

- Post-Exilic Prophets:
  Haggai, Zechariah, Malachi.

f. ***Prophets of the Interadvent Period*** *(400 B.C.—33 A.D.)*

- John the Baptist (Luke 1:76)
- Zacharias (Luke 1:67)
- Anna, a prophetess (Luke 2:36)
- Christ (John 6:14; Luke 4:24 cf. Isaiah 61:1)

g. ***New Testament Church Prophets*** *(33–100 A.D.)*

- Numerous anonymous prophets of the New Testament Church (Acts 11:27)
- Agabus (Acts 11:27–28)
- Barnabas (Acts 13:1)
- Simeon (Niger) (Acts 13:1)
- Lucius of Cyrene (Acts 13:1)
- Manaen (Acts 13:1)
- Judas (Acts 15:32)
- Silas (Acts 15:32)

It also seems evident that at least some of the Apostles were also prophets.

h. Prophets of the Present Age *(33 A.D.—Second Coming of Christ)*

Prophets continue in this age until Christ's Second Coming (Ephesians 4:11–14; 1 Corinthians 12:28).

Description of False Prophets

There are at least thirty references in the Old Testament to false prophets prophesying. These false prophets do not in reality speak for Jehovah but are speaking in their own name, things which they themselves have concocted. False prophecy is presumptuously speaking for God.

Old Testament Descriptive Word for False Prophecy

Zed. "Presume." A Hebrew word used in the Old Testament as descriptive of false prophecy is *ziyd.*

Deuteronomy 18:20, "But the prophet, which shall *presume (ziyd)* to speak a word in my name, which I have not commanded him to speak…."

The Hebrew word *ziyd* means "to boil up" or "to seethe."[36] The same Hebrew word is used in the verb form in some passages in the sense of something prepared by cooking (Genesis 25:29). Thus the false prophet is "boiling up" something to say. This is in direct contrast with the true prophet whose prophecy simply "bubbles up" (*naba*). The false prophecy must be made to "boil up" while the true prophecy "bubbles up." The false prophet "cooks it up" while the true prophet has it "gushing up" (*naba*) from within him.

Classes of False Prophets

There were two classes of false prophets in Israel (Deuteronomy 18:20).

a. Those false prophets who spake in the name of other gods

These false prophets would advocate going after other gods (Deuteronomy 13:2). Such prophets were soundly rejected and deserving of death (Deuteronomy 13:5).

b. Those false prophets who spoke falsely in Jehovah's name

The former group was easily discerned by their claim to speak for another god. The latter group, however, was much more difficult to detect as false. Certain tests must be applied to distinguish them from true prophets.

Characteristics of False Prophets

False prophets may be detected by their character and conduct. A false prophet will live a sinful and wicked life, while a true prophet will exemplify conduct and character which are consistent with God's character. A false prophet will bring forth evil fruit, and a true prophet will display good fruit.

Matthew 7:15–17, "Beware of false prophets, which come to you in sheep's clothing, but inwardly they are ravening wolves. Ye shall know them by their fruits. Do men gather grapes of thorns, or figs of thistles? Even so every good tree bringeth forth good fruit, but a corrupt tree bringeth forth evil fruit."

The lives of prophets thus attest to their spiritual authority. False prophets will reveal the following characteristics:

a. Ungodliness in attitudes

False prophets will reveal evil attitudes. These attitudes are a reflection of their perverted nature.

- Frivolous and light (Jeremiah 23:32; Zephaniah 3:4)
- Treacherous (Zephaniah 3:4)
- Opportunistic (Isaiah 30:10–11; Micah 2:11)
- Reckless (Isaiah 28:7)
- Violent (Matthew 7:15)
- Covetous (2 Peter 2:3)
- Presumptuous (2 Peter 2:10)
- Self-willed (2 Peter 2:10)
- Rebellious (2 Peter 2:10)
- Despising authority (2 Peter 2:10; Jude 8)
- Unwilling to listen to others (1 John 4:1, 6)
- Irreverent (Jude 4)
- Shameless (Jude 15)
- Mocking others (Jude 18)
- Spirit of superiority (Jude 19)
- Murmuring and complaining (Jude 16)

b. Ungodliness in appetites

False prophets are characterized in Scripture as of low morality. Their desires are perverted and base.

- Profane (Jeremiah 23:11)
- Greedy (Micah 3:5,11)
- Immoral (Jeremiah 23:15; 2 Peter 2:2)
- Degenerate (Zechariah 13:1–6; Matthew 7:15–20)
- Unclean (2 Peter 2:10)
- Lascivious (Jude 4)
- Lustful (Jude 18)

c. *Ungodliness in actions*

The evil deeds of the false prophets are the result of their evil hearts. Their works reflect their spiritual depravity. The source of their activity is shown to be unclean or evil spirits (1 Kings 22:19ff; Zechariah 13:1–6).

- Prophesied false revelation (Jeremiah 14:14; Ezekiel 22:28)
- Drunkards (Isaiah 28:7)
- Wickedness (Jeremiah 23:11)
- Conspired to deceive (Ezekiel 22:25; 2 Peter 2:3)
- Defrauded others (Ezekiel 22:25)
- Committed adultery (Jeremiah 23:14)
- Liars (Isaiah 9:15; Jeremiah 23:14, 32)
- Supported other evildoers (Jeremiah 23:14)
- Practiced divination (Jeremiah 14:14; Ezekiel 22:28)
- Evil speaking (2 Peter 2:12)
- False doctrine (1 John 4:1–2)

Figures of False Prophets

The following imagery is used as figures for the false prophets:

a. *Dogs*

- Dumb dogs (Isaiah 56:10)
- Greedy dogs (Isaiah 56:11)
- A dog turned to its own vomit (2 Peter 2:22)

b. *Ignorant shepherds* (Isaiah 56:11)

c. *The wind* (Jeremiah 5:13)

d. ***Slippery ways in the darkness*** (Jeremiah 23:12)

e. ***Chaff*** (Jeremiah 23:28)

f. ***Foxes in the deserts*** (Ezekiel 13:4)

g. ***Lions***

- A roaring lion ravening the prey (Ezekiel 22:25)
- A destroying lion (Jeremiah 2:30)

h. ***A fool*** (Hosea 9:7)

i. ***The snare of a fowler*** (Hosea 9:8)

j. ***Ravening wolves*** (Matthew 7:15)

The parallel passages of 2 Peter 2 and the Book of Jude are very graphic in their description of false ministries, especially the false prophet. Both introduce their figurative descriptions with references to Balaam, the classic Old Testament example of a false prophet (2 Peter 2:15–16; cf. 2:1; Jude 11).

k. ***Wells with no water*** (empty, 2 Peter 2:17)

l. ***Clouds carried with a tempest*** (promise but do not produce rain, 2 Peter 2:17)

m. ***Mists driven past by a squall of wind*** (unstable, 2 Peter 2:17)

n. ***Sunken rocks*** (dangerous, Jude 12)[37]

o. ***Perverted shepherds*** (selfish, Jude 12)

p. ***Rainless clouds*** (useless, Jude 12)

q. ***Barren trees*** (dead, Jude 12)

r. ***Foaming sea*** (carrying rubbish, Jude 13)

s. ***Wandering stars*** (doomed, Jude 13)

Descriptions of True Prophets

Titles of True Prophets

The titles given to prophets were depictive of them and their ministry. These titles were descriptive designations, not rising to the rank of formal names. They characterized the true prophet in his prophetic ministry.

a. Servant of the Lord. This title was descriptive of the prophet's close relation to the Lord in his ministry. He was the Lord's servant.

This title stressed the faithfulness and servile character of the prophet's ministry. The term seemed to emphasize that as God's spokesman, the prophet was doing God's work and fulfilling His purposes in the world. A familiar expression is "My servants the prophets" (2 Kings 9:7; 17:13; Jeremiah 7:25; Ezekiel–38:17; Zechariah 1:6). The title was one of high designation.

b. Messenger of the Lord. This title was descriptive of the prophet's relation to the people. They were those sent by God to deliver a message to others. This term was descriptive of the prophet's function. The same Hebrew term was used of angels as God's messengers. The prophets are viewed as "messengers" (Haggai 1:13; 2 Chronicles 36:15–16; Isaiah 44:26; Malachi 3:1).

c. Man of God. This term designated the prophet in relation to his personal character. In contrast to the perverse character of false prophets, the true prophet was God's holy man. It was used of the prophets Moses (Deuteronomy 33:1), Samuel (1 Samuel 9:6), Elijah (1 Kings 17:18, 20), and Elisha (2 Kings 4:7, 9).

d. Man of the Spirit. This title suggested the prophet in relation to his source of revelation. He was a man, moved upon by God's Spirit. This title is found in Hosea 9:7, "the prophet..., the spiritual man (Hebrew, *ish haruach*, literally, "man of the Spirit"). The term is also descriptive of the New Testament prophet (1 Corinthians 14:37).

e. Anointed one. This term depicted the prophet in relation to his holy calling. He was commissioned and anointed to his office, thus called of God to his prophetic ministry. This title is used of the prophets in 1 Chronicles 16:22 and Psalms 105:15.

f. Seer. This title has been treated in depth above. It was designative of the prophet in relation to his reception of God's revelation. The prophet must "see" before he would speak a prophetic word. Several usages of this term are 1 Samuel 9:9; 2 Samuel 24:11; 1 Chronicles 29:29; 2 Chronicles 29:25; Amos 7:12.

Figures of True Prophets

The following figures are used of true prophets of God:

a. Shepherds (Isaiah 56:11; Ezekiel 34:2–8)

This figure designated the prophet in his pastoral occupation as a voice, beckoning a flock of sheep. The prophet was given charge to go to the sheep fold and call to them a message from God.

b. The stay and the staff (Isaiah 3:1–2)

This figure of the prophets was not exclusive of them but included other leaders of the people (3:2–3). It described the prophet as a prop which was used of God in his ministry as a support to hold up the people.[38]

c. Bread and water (Isaiah 3:1–2)

This figure was also inclusive of the general leaders of Judah, including the prophet. It depicted the prophet in his role as a main support of Judah's very existence. He was "bread and water" to Judah and was a feeder of God's word to them.

d. ***A watchman*** *(Isaiah 21:6,11; Ezekiel 3:17; 33:2)*

This term is the most frequently used of all the true prophet's figures. This image likened the prophet to a sentinel on a wall whose duty was to alert the people of the dangers approaching them. As faithful watchmen, the prophets warned the people of spiritual peril facing them.

e. ***A trumpet blowing*** *(Isaiah 58:1; Jeremiah 6:17; Ezekiel 33:3–7; 1 Corinthians 14:8)*

This image described the prophet as sounding an alarm to warn the people. It viewed the prophet's role as a signal to arouse the people to action.

f. ***Prosecutor in the heavenly court*** *(Jeremiah 11:20; Micah 7:9)*

As God's spokesman, the prophet is pictured as a prosecutor in the Court of Heaven, presenting the case before God as judge. As prosecutor of the King's court, he brings to bear before heaven and earth the witness of the Mosaic law against the transgressions of the people. Many of the prophetic messages, therefore, took on the form of forensic accusations as familiarly used in the prosecutions of the Near Eastern courts.

The familiar Hebrew and Semitic term *riyb* is used of the prophets in their prophetic presentations. This Hebrew term regularly was used of a court prosecutor in his listing of legal violations. This Hebrew term *riyb* is used of the following prophet's declarations: David as prophet (1 Samuel 24:15; Psalms 43:1), Isaiah (Isaiah 34:8); Jeremiah (Jeremiah 11:20); Ezekiel (Ezekiel 44:24); Hosea (Hosea 4:1; 2:2); and Micah (Micah 6:2; 7:9).

g. ***A lion roaring*** *(Amos 3:7–8)*

The prophet's voice is likened to a lion's roar, bringing fear to the people so that they may respond to God. Also the prophet's role as a roaring lion may indicate imminent judgment and destruction.

The Prophetess

In Scripture, women are not excluded from the prophetic office. There are numerous examples of women called of God to the office as a prophetess (Hebrew, *neby'ah*). In these instances the prophetess may be seen as speaking or singing prophetically.

a. *The false prophetess*

- There were false prophetesses in Ezekiel's time who deceived the people and supported, with their prophetic utterances, the wicked (Ezekiel 13:17–22).
- Noadiah, a prophetess during the restoration period, was aligned with Nehemiah's opposition (Nehemiah 6:14).
- Jezebel was a false prophetess, pictured in the Book of Revelation (Revelation 2:20).

b. *The true prophetess*

- Miriam, the sister of Moses, was a prophetess (Exodus 15:20).
- Deborah, a judge of Israel, was a prophetess (Judges 4:4), who sang prophetic songs (Judges 5:2–31).
- Hannah, while not called a prophetess, uttered a beautiful prophecy (1 Samuel 2:1–10).
- Isaiah's wife was called a prophetess (Isaiah 8:2–3).
- Huldah, was a prophetess, consulted by the high priest at the command of King Josiah (2 Kings 22:14).
- Anna was a New Testament prophetess (Luke 2:36–38).
- The four daughters of Philip the Evangelist prophesied, although the term "prophetess" is not directly used of them.
- The Corinthian church expected the regular prophetic ministry of the prophetess (1 Corinthians 11:5).

Women are called today by God to the prophetic office of a prophetess. A prophetess may operate in a presbytery as well as a prophet. This will be further discussed below.

THE FUNCTION OF THE PROPHETIC WORD

The prophetic word serves many varied purposes. Its function is vital to the spiritual growth both of the individual believer and the corporate assembly.

THE FUNCTION OF PROPHECY IN A PRESBYTERY

The various functions of prophecy in a presbytery are as broad as the functions of the office of a prophet. Therefore, it becomes obvious that the forming of a presbytery should include those who are proven prophets. This does not mean that all of these functions will occur in every prophetic word, but that every word will include at least one or a combination of these functions.

Edification

1 Corinthians 14:3, "But he that prophesieth speaketh unto men to edification...."

The word "edification" indicates the *building up* of the believer in his spiritual life. Prophecy increases faith and spiritual understanding. It edifies by bringing growth towards spiritual maturity.

The Old Testament prophet sought to edify God's people. The prophets purposed through their messages to build up the people in their spiritual relationship to Jehovah. The Apostle Paul emphasized the truth that New Testament prophecy edifies the Body of Christ in 1 Corinthians 14 (vss. 4, 5, 6, 22, 24, and 31).

Exhortation

1 Corinthians 14:3, "But he that prophesieth speaketh unto men to... exhortation...."

Exhortation comprises the admonition and warning aspects of prophecy. This function of prophecy serves to keep the believer from straying away from God.

Exhortation also includes the idea of encouragement, a stirring of the believer from that which would spiritually stagnate him. The prophets exhorted God's people by warning them of the dangerous consequences of continued sin. The New Testament prophets, Judas and Silas, ministered in this prophetic function at Antioch:

Acts 15:32, "And Judas and Silas, being prophets also themselves, exhorted the brethren with many words, and confirmed them."

Comfort

1 Corinthians 14:3, "But he that prophesieth speaketh unto men to... comfort."

Comfort is the consolation which the prophetic word brings in times of affliction, trials, and persecution. The Comforter, the Holy Spirit, prompts the prophetic word to comfort those in suffering or troubles. So the prophet Isaiah bore a message of comfort to the faithful remnant in difficult times in the latter half of his book (chapters 40–66).

These three functions of prophecy operate in all the realms of prophecy, the spirit, the gift, and the office of prophecy. The following six functions of prophecy should operate only on the level of proven prophets or other five-fold ministries of Ephesians 4:11–12.

Direction

The Old Testament prophets at times gave divine direction to God's people. Samuel directed Saul, saying to him:

> 1 Samuel 10:8, "And thou shalt go down before me to Gilgal, and behold, I will come down unto thee...."

So also Elisha prophesied a word of direction to the woman whose son he had restored to life:

> 2 Kings 8:1, "...Arise, and go thou and thine household, and sojourn wheresoever thou canst sojourn: for the Lord hath called for a famine; and it shall also come upon the land seven years."

In the New Testament the presbytery held at Antioch is an example of direction. There were prophets and teachers gathered together there. After a time of prayer and fasting, God spoke a word of direction concerning His timing for the separation of Barnabas and Saul from that body for release to a more mobile ministry. The word also included confirmation of their previous callings.

> Acts 13:1–2, "Now there were in the church that was at Antioch certain prophets and teachers. As they ministered to the Lord, and fasted, the Holy Ghost said, 'Separate me Barnabas and Saul for the work whereunto I have called them.'"

a. The prophetic word as military orders. Paul stated in 1 Timothy 1:18, "This *charge* I commit unto thee, son Timothy, according to the prophecies which went before on thee, that thou by them mightest war a good warfare."

The Greek word for "charge," *paraggelia,* was used as a military term in biblical times. It indicated the military orders or directions given to a soldier by a superior. Paul was fond of military metaphors. Here, it is an obvious reference, according to the Greek grammatical construction[39], to the time of Timothy's laying on of hands and prophecies by the presbytery (cf. 1 Timothy 4:14).

At this time, Timothy received clear directions regarding his pastoral call at Ephesus and its challenge to oppose heresy and establish the people in sound doctrine (see 1 Timothy 1:3, 5 where the same Greek word is consciously used by Paul). These were apparently the directions of his military orders as a good soldier of Jesus Christ, and he was to war by them.

When a believer presents himself as a candidate before a presbytery, he is in a sense "reporting for duty" as a soldier of Christ Jesus. As the prophetic word flows, he receives his military orders, so that he may now go forth to war a good warfare.

b. The means of directional revelation. Direction or guidance is largely a manifestation of the Holy Spirit's gift of the word of wisdom (1 Corinthians 12:8).

> Ephesians 1:17–18, "That the God of our Lord Jesus Christ, the Father of glory, may give unto you the spirit of wisdom and revelation…that ye may know what is the hope of His calling…."

Paul is praying that the spirit will grant them the word of wisdom and such revelation in order that they may come better to know God's calling (a purpose clause in Greek syntax, showing that direction regarding this calling would further come through the spirit of wisdom and revelation). The fact that such gifts are operative today would suggest that this would be expected at times in the prophetic flow of a presbytery.

> 1 Corinthians 14:29–30, "Let the prophets speak two or three, and let the other judge. If any thing be *revealed* to another that sitteth by, let the first hold his peace."

The function of direction again warrants a further word of caution. Only proven prophets and mature ministries should ever function in this prophetic dimension.

Conferral

Not only is there the pronouncement of spiritual gifts and ministries through prophecy in a presbytery, but there may be also the conferral of the same through the prophetic word.

> 1 Timothy 4:14, "Neglect not the gift that is in thee, which was given thee *by prophecy*, with the laying on of the hands of the presbytery."

As mentioned above, the spiritual gift that Timothy received was granted to him *"by* prophecy." The preposition "by" (Greek, *dia*) literally means "through," revealing that which is shown to be a channel. Paul is saying that prophecy was a channel "through" which the spiritual gift was conferred upon Timothy (see above, "The Causative Aspect of Prophecy"). This verse and 2 Timothy 1:6 both show that the laying on of hands also coupled together with the prophetic word act as dual channels for the conferral of this gift.

Confirmation

Much of the content of presbytery prophecies will be a confirming word of what God has already revealed, at least in part, to the candidates.

Confirmation is necessary to establish a word (2 Corinthians 13:1).

The prophet Agabus prophesied after binding his hands and feet with Paul's girdle:

> Acts 21:11, "…Thus saith the Holy Ghost, 'So shall the Jews at Jerusalem bind the man that owneth this girdle, and shall deliver him into the hands of the Gentiles.'"

This prophecy was a confirming word of Ananias' previous revelation that God would show Paul the great things he must suffer for Christ's name (Acts 9:16).

The prophetic ministry of the prophets Judas and Silas in Asia Minor was mostly confirming in function.

> Acts 15:32, 41, "And Judas and Silas, being prophets also themselves, exhorted the brethren with many words, and *confirmed* them.… And he went through Syria and Cilicia, *confirming* the churches."

Paul makes a cryptic but yet obvious reference to a presbytery in Corinth, the details of which would be unknown, in which gifts were imparted (cf. 1 Timothy 4:14), prophetic utterances functioned to confirm, and the word of knowledge was operating in revelation.

> 1 Corinthians 1:4–7, "I thank my God always on your behalf…that in every thing ye are enriched by him, in all *utterance,* and in all *knowledge*; even as the testimony of Christ was confirmed in you: so that ye come behind in no gift…."

Paul's reference here is a statement of his thankfulness that these gifts are flowing in the Corinthian body even as they did on the occasion of this former presbytery.

Correction

A corrective word is one which is a message of setting right, a chastening word, or a call to repentance. It is never delivered in harshness but in loving reproof.

The prophets repeatedly brought prophetic messages which were corrective words. Several examples will illustrate this function:

- Amos' prophetic visions (locusts, fire, the plumbline, a basket of summer fruit, and the Lord standing upon the altar (chapters 7–9) were corrective.
- Micah's prophetic appeals to the corrupt leadership (chapters 3–6) were corrective.
- The prophetic calls of Haggai and Zechariah to stir the people from defeat and lethargy to completion of the new temple were corrective.
- Malachi's prophetic oracles to unfaithful messengers, guilty of hypocrisy and insincerity, were corrective words.
- The Apostle Paul described a didactic service of prophecy:

1 Corinthians 14:31, "For ye may all prophesy one by one, that all may *learn....*"

Prophecy causes one to "learn." The Greek word here for "learn" *(manthaneo)* means not only instructive learning but also corrective learning. The same Greek word is used in the corrective sense in 1 Corinthians 4:6 and Titus 3:14.

Judgment

One of the major themes of the Old Testament prophets was judgment for continued and unrepentant sin. Judgment was basically restorative in purpose, not punitive.

- Some prophets centered their judgments almost entirely upon heathen nations: Jonah—Nineveh; Nahum—Nineveh; Obadiah—Edom.
- Some prophets centered their judgments almost entirely upon God's own people: Hosea—Israel; Joel—Judah; Micah—Israel and Judah, the only prophet to address his messages to both nations.
- Some prophets proclaimed judgment both on God's people and the surrounding heathen nations: Isaiah, Jeremiah, and Amos.

- Some prophets interpreted judgment to the people: Habakkuk emphasized the integrity of God's judgments; Jeremiah emphasized the righteousness of God's judgments; Ezekiel emphasized the justice of God's judgments; Daniel emphasized the sovereignty of God in His judgments.

New Testament prophets are the successors of the Old Testament prophets. Proven prophets today may function in judgment. We see prophetic insight in the judgments of Paul (1 Corinthians 5:5; 1 Timothy 1:20).

Equipping of the Saints

Ephesians 4:11–12 states that the five-fold ministries, including the prophet, serve to "equip" or "perfect" the saints:

Ephesians 4:11–12, "And he gave some, apostles; and some prophets.... For the perfecting (equipping) of the saints, for the work of the ministry...."

This word "perfect" (equip) in the Greek is *katartismos*. It is a compound of the Greek term, *kata*, meaning "a standard by which judgment may be passed," and *artismos,* meaning "to repair, to adjust, to fashion or work with the hands as craftsman."

The "equipping" of the saints then is the fashioning or setting in order of the lives of believers, based upon a judgment of their relation to God's standard, the written Word of God.

In a presbytery, God gives a word to fashion and adjust the candidates as He judges their relation to His divine standard. As a result, they may be set in order and equipped themselves to do the work of ministry.

Responding to Presbytery Prophecies

Spiritual preparation for a presbytery is vital to properly responding to the prophetic word when it comes. After the presbytery is over, the candidate is also responsible for maintaining proper responses to the word *which he* received.

Improper responses are subtle and can quickly creep into a person's life if he does not continue the same spiritual intensity. There is a temptation to relax spiritually after a presbytery is over. If the candidate does not continue to press into God as he did during the presbytery, improper responses can soon appear.

Proper Responses

a. Faith

Receiving the prophetic word in faith

Hebrews 11:6, "Faith is essential in receiving anything from God. As the candidate asks God for a word, he must ask in faith."

James 1:6–7, "But let him ask in *faith,* nothing wavering. For he that wavereth is like a wave of the sea driven with the wind and tossed. For let not that man think that he shall receive any thing of the Lord."

The candidate who has faith in his heart will have an excitement and an anticipation that God will speak to him what he needs to hear from God. There will be a confidence in God to fulfill all that He has spoken, if the candidate cooperates with God's plan for his life.

2 Chronicles 20:20, "…believe his prophets, so shall ye prosper."

Galations 3:2, "…Received ye the Spirit by the works of the law, or by the *hearing of faith?*"

The testing of a word from God

It is the way of God to test the word that He brings. Every word from God will be tested.

Psalms 18:30, "As for God, his way is perfect: the word of the Lord is tried: he is buckler to all those that trust in him." (cf. 2 Samuel 22:31).

Psalms 12:6, "The words of the Lord are pure words: as silver tried in a furnace of earth…."

The testing of the prophetic word is a test of faith. One of the laws of God in His kingdom is the law of faith. As God has put natural laws in the order of the physical universe, so He has established spiritual laws in his kingdom.

- **The law of faith** (Romans 3:27)

*The law of faith operates in four consecutive steps. The cycle of these four steps are a regular pattern in God's dealings with His people. Once a word is received from God, this cycle is set in motion by God.

1. *The creation of faith: receiving a word from God*

Not only must the prophetic word be received in faith, but a word from God births further faith in the heart of the presbytery candidate. Faith is created by the hearing and receiving of the word.

Romans 10:17, "So then faith cometh by hearing, and hearing by a word of God."

2. *The compliance of faith: obeying the word from God*

As the word is received with confirmation, the candidate must have a willing spirit to obey God's word and do what He has said. He willingly cooperates with God's word to do his part.

James 1:22, "But be ye doers of the word, and not hearers only, deceiving your own selves."

3. *The crisis of faith: the testing of the word from God*

Now the prophetic word is tested as there comes a crisis of faith. The crisis will often appear in circumstances which would seem to contradict the fulfillment of the word. The evidence will suggest that this former word could never be realized. Others often misunderstand the person's steadfastness of faith, as faith in the word from God is put to a severe test.

4. *The consequence of faith: The fulfillment of the word from God*

After a season of testing, God fulfills the word which he had spoken. Faith, having been tried by the testing of the word, now sees its reward with the fulfillment by God of the prior word.

- **Scriptural examples of God testing the Word**

Numerous biblical examples illustrate this principle. One example each from the Old Testament and New Testament will demonstrate this manner of God's dealings.

1. Joseph (Genesis 37–45)

Joseph dreamed two dreams from God which prophetically foreshadowed a time when he would be established as a ruler and his father, mother, and brethren would bow down before him. Thus Joseph received an unusual word from God for a youth who was 17 years of age.

There soon came a testing of the word as Joseph was sold into slavery in Egypt and put unjustly in prison. His circumstances seemed to contradict all possibility of fulfillment of the word. Yet God in his time fulfilled that word as Joseph became a ruler in Egypt, and his brethren came to Egypt in a time of famine, bowing down before him.

2. Saul of Tarsus (Apostle Paul)

God gave a word through Ananias that Saul of Tarsus would "...bear my name before the Gentiles, and kings...." (Acts 9:15–16). After receiving this word and accepting it in faith, a testing of that word soon came as Saul had to escape from Damascus at the peril of his life (Acts 9:23–26). He was beaten and imprisoned repeatedly. It appeared that there was no way possible that he would bear the Lord's name before Gentiles and kings.

Yet after the severe testing of the word, this word was fulfilled as Saul, now Paul, travelled on three missionary journeys to Gentile lands (Acts 13:4–21:17). He also witnessed before Felix (Acts 24:26–27); Festus (Acts 25:11–12), and King Agrippa (Acts 26).

b. Humility

The prophetic word must be received in a spirit of humility. Some times a candidate will have preconceived ideas of a great ministry that he believes God will speak to him in a presbytery. When God doesn't confirm his ideas of great importance, he is disillusioned, depressed, and angry at God and the presbyters, who he believes missed the mind of God.

The candidate must rather approach a presbytery in a humble spirit which says, "Whatever is your will, Oh God, I will gladly accept and do."

God will on occasion unveil a future ministry of significant importance to a candidate. He must humbly accept this word without allowing himself to become puffed up or exalted in his own eyes.

Psalms 34:2, "…the humble shall *hear thereof,* and be glad."

James 4:10, "Humble yourselves in the sight of the Lord, and he shall lift you up."

c. *Meekness*

The presbytery candidate should receive the prophetic word with a spirit of meekness.

James 1:21, "…and receive *with meekness th*e engrafted word."

Meekness is strength under control. The Greek word for "meekness," *praus,* was used in New Testament times to describe a wild horse which had been tamed, now under the control of the bit and bridle. The beast had not lost its strength, but rather the strength had been brought under control of another.[40] Meekness is the taming of our restless spirit, brought under the control of God.

A spirit of meekness acknowledges the sovereign control of God over the life and future ministry of the individual. It does not seek to push a ministry which may have been mentioned in a prophetic word. It does not try to force the ministry in one's own power, but allows God to develop the ministry. It is willing to let God cause the ministry to surface without prematurely rushing off to fulfill a ministry in one's own strength.

d. *Patience*

One of the hardest things after a presbytery is patiently waiting for God to bring to pass that which he has spoken. Many times there is a period of years before the fulfillment of portions of the prophetic word are realized.

The principle of delay is one of the tests of the prophetic word which we may expect. We can learn much through delay, and this instruction, through God, saves time and never loses it. Delay will hasten the steps of anointed service, if received in a patient spirit.

Romans 8:25, "But if we hope for that we see not, then do we *with patience* wait for it."

James 1:3, "Knowing this, that the trying of your faith worketh *patience.*"

e. Joy

The presbytery candidate should respond to the prophetic word with a spirit of rejoicing. Some times the Holy Spirit will bring a corrective word or probe deep into the inner spirit to speak to a hidden need. The word, however, must be received with joy, knowing that God is strengthening and fashioning us for His glory.

Some individuals in their presbytery prophecies may have ministries mentioned over them which seem to exceed in importance those mentioned over you. You must rejoice with them and thank God for their future ministry. You should also accept with joy God's position for you in the body of Christ.

1 Corinthians 12:26, "And whether one member suffer, all the members suffer with it; or one member be honoured, all the members rejoice with it."

God does not always value different ministries on levels as we do. All ministries are important and necessary in God's House.

1 Peter 1:8, "...ye rejoice with joy unspeakable and full of glory."

f. Submission

The candidate should have a submissive spirit to the local church leadership who now are responsible to guide him in the revealed purposes of God for his life. He must allow his pastor to be a voice to him and seek his counsel. He should accept the leadership's judgments in opening opportunities for his ministry to function.

Hebrews 13:17, "Obey them that have the rule over you, and submit yourselves: for they watch for your souls, as they that must give account, and they may do it with joy, and not with grief: for that is unprofitable for you."

Improper Responses

One should always remember that the prophetic word is conditional upon the individual's response to God and his word. Improper responses may hinder or prevent the fulfillment of God's purposes in his life.

a. Doubt

Many different doubts can rush in upon an individual during a presbytery and after it. There can be doubts that God will speak to the candidate, doubts that he is ready and worthy to have God speak to him, doubts that he could ever do what God has spoken, doubts that he has really heard from God rather than man, and many others. These doubts must be rejected and faith must rise to believe God in all things.

Matthew 14:31, "O thou of little faith, wherefore didst thou doubt?"

Luke 12:29, "...neither be ye of doubtful mind."

Hebrews 4:2 "...the word preached did not profit them because those who heard it, did not combine it with faith."

b. Pride

When God speaks prophetically to indicate a future ministry of importance or to honor or commend the individual, he must not allow his ego to become inflated. Pride will eventually destroy the ministry and its potential that God had spoken to him in the presbytery. Pride will cause him to rely upon himself rather than God for strength.

c. Anger

One must never become angry at God for not saying what the candidate wanted to hear. Such a response in any form is indicative of something wrong in the heart of the individual. Wrath is not pleasing to God and can rob the candidate of all that God had purposed to do through the prophetic word.

d. Bitterness

Bitterness usually comes as a result of disappointment. Its roots are a self-centered spirit. The person may be bitter at God for not giving him a higher position in the body of Christ or bitter because God openly exposed some areas in his life that needed to be changed. Bitterness will likewise destroy and must be uprooted out of the heart.

James 3:14–15, "But if ye have bitter envying...this wisdom descendeth not from above, but is earthly, sensual, devilish."

e. Independent spirit

An independent spirit can bring to ruin that which God has spoken in a presbytery prophecy. The individual's refusal to submit himself to the guidance of the local leadership leaves him without checks and balances in his spiritual growth. Because of lack of wisdom and inexperience, he will make mistakes which could injure others as well as himself.

God will not bless a rebellious individual nor allow that ministry to properly see its fruitfulness ordained for it. Such an individual becomes dangerous rather than profitable to the church.

Psalms 66:7, "…let not the rebellious exalt themselves."

Psalms 68:6, "…the rebellious dwell in a dry land."

f. Jealousy

Jealousy over important ministries which God has spoken to others must be dealt with at once. This response is a self-centered problem. It can bring disunity amidst God's people and havoc in the person's own heart. Jealousy and envy must be eradicated from the individual as he realizes that all of God's blessings are given on the basis of His grace.

Proverbs 6:34, "For jealousy is the rage of a man…."

Song of Solomon 8:6, "…jealousy is cruel as the grave: the coals thereof are coals of fire, which hath a most vehement flame."

- Section Three -

Procedures of a Presbytery

Prophecy and the laying on of hands of the presbytery is a ministry to strengthen a local body of believers. For a local church to enter into the full blessings of the ministry of a presbytery, it is important to have an understanding of the practical functioning of the presbytery and the presbytery services.

THE PRESBYTERS

The Description of a Presbyter

A presbyter is someone who is one of the governmental ministries in the body of Christ. The presbyter may be one of the five-fold ministries of Ephesians 4:11, apostle, prophet, evangelist, pastor, and teacher.

The word "presbyter" comes from the Greek word *presbuteros*, translated "elder" most often in the New Testament. This Greek word is descriptive of the man himself who is an elder, rather than his eldership function which is indicated by another Greek term for "elder" *(episkopos).*

The Greek term *presbuteros* carried a connotation of one who is mature, both in the natural personality and the spiritual man. Therefore, a presbyter in a presbytery should not be a novice in spiritual things (1 Timothy 3:6). Also if he is to function as a peer presbyter in the presbytery, he should not be a "novice" in the prophetic realm nor in functioning in a presbytery. Younger and immature prophetic ministries can operate from time to time in a presbytery, but they should be accompanied by a more senior presbyter with whom the younger ministry is being tutored and developed in his ministry in a Timothy manner. The younger and more inexperienced prophetic ministry should hold back some in the prophetic flow of a presbytery until his gift has developed with more maturity and proven itself.

Since the word "presbyter" (Gk., *presbuteros*) emphasized the maturity of the man who is a presbyter, the presbyter should evidence the following characteristics:

1. A presbyter should ideally be an elder in his own home local church. Since the word "presbyter" means "elder," this would seem to be an obvious implication. A presbyter should be one whose maturity has been proven in his life and in his ministry. Therefore, as an elder in his own local church body, he has proven himself among those who would know him best.

2. The presbyter should qualify according to all the character requirements of 1 Timothy 3:1–7.

3. The presbyter should have high moral standards and live a life in true holiness. He should be blameless (1 Timothy 3:2). One who is careless in these vital areas brings the prophetic realm into disrepute by the reproach of his life, disqualifies himself, and is dangerous because he cannot be a pure channel of God's revelation.

4. The presbyter should not be influenced by money. The advantage of financial gain must not govern him in any manner as to his prophetic ministry. He must have pure motivations.

The false prophets of Israel were guilty in this area of personal greed (Micah 3:11). False prophets today will be greatly concerned with financial benefits for themselves in their ministry.

5. The presbyter should be doctrinally sound (1 Timothy 1:18–19; 4:16).

6. The presbyter should evidence the residency of the gift of prophecy in his life (1 Corinthians 12:10). While he need not be called to the prophetic office as a prophet, he should be able to flow regularly in the prophetic gift.

The Nature of a Presbytery

A presbytery must be composed of at least two or more presbyters. A presbytery ideally, however, should have three or four presbyters.

No one ministry has all revelation (1 Corinthians 12:7,11). One presbyter would not usually have the whole of what God would desire to say to the candidate. Three presbyters will usually give a more thorough and rounded prophetic picture than one presbyter.

It is God's way to have every word confirmed in the mouth of two or three witnesses (2 Corinthians 13:1). The plurality of a presbytery also minimizes the danger of one man being elevated too highly in the eyes of the people.

A presbytery which has three or four strong prophetic ministries would not need to have more presbyters. More presbyters will usually contribute only further words of prophetic confirmation which have little new content. Much longer time will be required for each candidate, and less people usually will have the opportunity to benefit from this ministry.

One of the presbyters should be designated as the senior of the presbytery. This would be determined before the presbytery meetings begin in conjunction with the local pastor. The senior presbyter should be the most mature and experienced of the presbyters. If one of the presbyters is a recognized apostle, he would often be a likely choice for the senior presbyter. The senior presbyter would be responsible in taking the leadership role among the presbyters as to direction regarding the presbytery meetings or any other considerations which may occur.

The Formation of a Presbytery

It is to be desired that a presbytery would include an apostle and a prophet among the presbyters. An apostle brings a mantle of strong authority and government into the presbytery. The prophetic mantle of the prophet is vital to insure a greater depth of prophetic revelation than may be operative from other presbyters who are not prophets.

In the formation of a presbytery, it is good to have at least one presbyter return, if possible, who has served in a former presbytery in that local church. He would be a familiar face who already has the confidence and respect of the people from the previous occasion. This should help to more quickly build rapport and confidence of the people with the presbytery. If this is the church's first presbytery, this would, of course, not be possible.

Likewise, it is also good to invite new presbyters who have never functioned as such in that particular local church. If a presbyter becomes too acquainted with the people, it can hinder his function in the prophetic realm.

Bringing in presbyters from other places outside the local church is the best procedure. It is possible for churches with mature ministries to have sufficient ministries resident to form a local presbytery. However, when other presbyters are brought in from outside the local church, they are not familiar with the people and their problems. These presbyters do not have to continually sort out in prophecy what they know from personal knowledge or revelation. Also, when God speaks prophetically in revelation, it has a greater impact on the people because they know that the presbyters do not know them. Local presbyters can still participate with the presbytery, but they would not assume the greater volume of prophetic ministry but would leave that to the visiting presbyters.

Acts 15:22, 32, "Then pleased it the apostles and elders, with the whole church, to send chosen men of their own company to Antioch with Paul and Barnabas, namely Judas surnamed Barsabbas, and Silas, chief men among the brethren.... And Judas and Silas, being prophets also themselves, exhorted the brethren with many words, and confirmed them."

Visiting presbyters do not usurp authority over the local leadership by virtue of their presence and function in a presbytery. The visiting presbyters are under the authority of the local leadership at all times. They must voluntarily submit to the authority of the local oversight who have the final decision in any matter of question. Since the local leaders are ultimately responsible before God for the souls of the people, they must be the ones who bear the final authority.

A presbytery may include a prophetess. It is not necessary, however, for every presbytery to have a prophetess. It is ideal to have a prophetess or female presbyter who functions with her husband, who would also be one of the presbyters.

The Preparation of a Presbytery for Prophetic Ministry

The presbyters will prepare themselves spiritually for the presbytery. Fasting and prayer prior to the presbytery meetings by the presbyters will usually result in a higher level of prophetic flow in presbytery services. There is increased in the presbyter by fasting and prayer a greater sensitivity to hear from God in revelation.

It is better that the fasting of a presbytery be done before the presbytery meetings and that the presbyters eat lightly during the days of the presbytery services to maintain their strength. Because the presbyters are guests of a local church, there is a tendency to want to feed them well with large and elaborate meals. However, light meals and snack foods are best for a presbytery season. Arrangements for eating can be discussed with the presbyters when they arrive at the beginning of a presbytery.

A presbyter should be told in advance of his coming what is expected of him in ministry other than the prophetic realm so that he may properly prepare. If he is to minister the Word, he should be told how many times he is expected to speak. However, this should be limited so as to not heavily burden the presbyters and distract them from their primary purpose for being there. Since the presbyters are there to primarily minister prophetically with the laying on of hands, it is unwise to overload them with too many other responsibilities, such as musical specials, song leading, taking offerings, or other similar things. Because of the nature of these meetings, such added responsibilities can be distracting and unnecessarily burdening to the presbyters.

During presbytery meetings the presbyter's time between services should not be scheduled too heavily. Extensive sight-seeing, numerous meetings with leadership, or counseling of difficult problem people in the church should be guarded against by the local pastor and only arranged at the willing consent of the presbyters. The presbyters should be allowed time for relaxation and maintaining a spirit of prayer.

The Function of a Presbytery

The presbyters will each prophesy over the candidate in turn. Sometimes a presbyter will receive a revelation which he feels would be better shared privately in counsel rather than prophesied publicly. Also a presbyter may see the need to counsel the candidate regarding the prophetic word which has just come over him. In both instances the presbyter will quietly share his counsel to the candidate as the other presbyters huddle together with him, adding their counsel briefly as needed. Although such counsel is required in certain instances, it should be kept in focus that this is a presbytery, not a counseling session.

When it is obvious that the presbyters have no further prophetic words to deliver to the candidate, one of the presbyters, usually the senior presbyter, will ask the presbyters now to pray over the candidate with the laying on of hands. As seen above, the act of laying on of hands of the presbytery is not just a formal ritual, but it is a significant time where spiritual activity is accomplished in the candidate through this act. Therefore, many presbyters ask the congregation to stand in recognition of the reverential seriousness of this time. The congregation would be asked to pray along with the presbytery for the candidate and the eventual fulfillment of God's purposes for his life.

A presbytery can function effectively only as long as the prophetic mantle is upon the presbytery. If this prophetic mantle would seem to lift and the prophetic flow becomes strained to the presbyters, the presbytery will usually stop and continue no further in that particular meeting. The prophetic flow of revelation cannot be forced.

If the presbyters become too physically exhausted or the atmosphere of congregational worship is weak, the prophetic mantle may lift from the presbytery. Therefore, it is not wise to presume to have a certain number of candidates for any one presbytery service. After only several candidates have been ministered to by the presbytery, it may appear unwise to continue to minister prophetically, and so the order of service will be changed to perhaps the ministry of the Word.

Sometimes, however, the spiritual tide is so high and the prophetic mantle so strong that the presbytery can continue to minister prophetically for several hours over candidates. Usually the senior presbyter will take the leadership in counsel with the other presbyters in the decision that the presbytery should not continue to minister prophetically any further in the service.

The congregation should be exhorted before a presbytery meeting to allow the presbytery alone to move in the prophetical realm in ministry over candidates. Because there is a prophetical mantle upon a presbytery, different people could often also minister a prophetic word from the congregation by means of the spirit of prophecy (see above). However, this should be strongly discouraged. This ministry is the reason why the presbytery has been formed and brought to the local church, and so it is best reserved for them. Also the congregational ministries are usually novices in the prophetical realm and should hold back and allow for the mature presbytery ministries to function.

Sometimes the presbytery will receive prophetic revelation regarding someone in the congregation who was not necessarily one of the candidates. They may call that party to come forward, and they will then minister prophetically over him. This does not happen often but God is sovereign and will occasionally so move in this manner.

The Function of a Presbytery in Larger Churches

As churches continue to grow and more people desire prophetic ministry, having more than one prophetic presbytery team will become a necessity.

Being a part of the leadership of a large mega-church in Portland, Oregon, we were faced with the reality of this as more and more people were desiring to go through prophetic presbytery at the same time. So, instead of putting potential candidates off for a year or two, we decided to make a transition by having multiple prophetic presbyteries going on at the same time. This allowed more people who were properly prepared to receive the vital ministry of the laying on of hands and prophecy.

As a large church we have a scheduled time for this ministry to happen. We have scheduled it at the end of January every year. Generally this would be a two to three day event, with multiple meetings in the morning afternoon and evening. We usually have this end with a Sunday night praise and prophetic night.

Those who desire this ministry would fill out the necessary application form, to receive prophetic presbytery, with their district/area pastor's approval, then they in turn would submit these lists to the elders, who would go over any questionable candidates. If there are no reservations in the eldership the person(s) are then put on the list to receive prophetic ministry.

We have any where from three to seven prophetic presbytery teams going on at the same time. Each team would have a person who acts as the team leader. We call him/her the team captain. This is usually one of our elders or district/area pastors. He/she is the one who would coordinate the ministers and the candidates.

On each of the teams would be a senior prophetic minister who would not be from the same local church. Other team members can be from the same local church. We have done this because many of the people in large churches do not know the candidates. This is important in keeping the integrity of the prophetic ministry over the candidates. So, our teams would have at least one to three visiting prophetic ministers and the rest of the team would be made up of gifted ministers of our own congregation.

We have been conducting these multiple teams and settings for several years now and hundreds of people have been blessed with the laying on of hands and prophecy in the local church.

THE CANDIDATES

The Qualifications of Presbytery Candidates

The ministry of prophecy and the laying on of hands of the presbytery must not be done on an indiscriminate basis. Candidates must be carefully selected as qualified for this ministry.

The Scriptures warn against a careless handling of presbytery functions:

1 Timothy 5:22, "Lay hands suddenly on no man, neither be partaker of other men's sins. Keep thyself pure."

This command warns us not to be in a hurry to lay hands on anyone. There must be due inquiry of their lives and the assurance of their qualification and readiness to receive this ministry. By allowing unqualified candidates to receive the ministry of a presbytery, we are excusing them from the prerequisite basics which comprise a proper spiritual foundation for a pure and prosperous life and ministry. Since laying on of hands involves identification, we can later become associated in the minds of others with their sins.

The following guidelines may be followed in judging the qualification of the candidates:

1. The candidate should be saved and know Jesus Christ as his personal Savior (John 3:7).

2. The candidate should be baptized in water by immersion (Acts 2:38).

3. The candidate should be already filled with the Holy Spirit (Ephesians 5:18).

These areas are obviously foundational in the spiritual life of the believer. If someone has not experienced all of these vital areas in his life, he should seek through God to have these areas realized in his life rather than seeking a prophetic word through the presbytery.

4. The candidate should be old enough to receive the prophetic word of God with maturity. Younger children should not be ministered to in a presbytery. There is plenty of time for this ministry later as they mature. A good minimum age is that the young person be at least in his last year of high school to be considered eligible for the ministry of a presbytery. At this time, young people often face major decisions as to the future direction of their lives.

5. The candidate should also evidence a degree of spiritual maturity. The candidate should reflect a stable, spiritual life, be faithful in attending the House of the Lord, and be submitted to local church leadership. This ministry is not intended to be therapeutic to those who are spiritually sick.

6. The candidate should have been in the local assembly for more than one year or at least a comparable time. This guards against someone coming into the church for a short period of time just before a presbytery for the sole purpose of being able to receive this ministry.

Also, any future ministry that God indicates to the candidate can only realize its proper and effective fulfillment in and through a local body. If the person is not solidly planted in the local assembly, the prophetic word will only bring subsequent frustration and eventual problems if he is trying to find this fulfillment in himself alone.

7. The candidate should be a member of the local congregation where the presbytery is held. If qualified believers from other local assemblies desire this ministry, it should be required that the candidate have the willing consent of his own pastor and that the pastor be present in the service to bear witness to the prophetic word. Since the pastor will have the continuous oversight responsibility for this individual and the prophetic word over him, he should also be there to hear what God would say to him.

Often there are more qualified candidates in a local church desirous for presbytery ministry than time will permit to receive this ministry in a particular series of meetings. Therefore, it is unwise to agree to have candidates from other churches, even with their pastors present except in certain, special cases.

8. If the local church has had the ministry of a presbytery before, the believer who has had this ministry previously should not present himself before the presbytery simply because this ministry is available once again to the church. The individual should not present himself again as a candidate until a number of years have passed during which he has fulfilled that which God has spoken to him in the previous word. Also, there should be a particular decision or consideration facing him about which he desires to hear from God.

Some people want to repeatedly have various prophecies come over them, but they are doing little in their lives to fulfill what God has previously spoken to them. The local leadership should guard against this happening in the congregation.

The Choosing of Candidates for a Presbytery

The local leadership bears the responsibility for choosing candidates for a presbytery upon the basis of the qualifications suggested above. No one should be forced to receive this ministry who does not desire it.

Those who are desirous for the ministry of a presbytery should make it known to the leadership. This may be done through either a verbal request, a sign-up sheet, the completing of an application form for presbytery ministry, or any other such procedure. It should be clearly made known to the people from the beginning that their expression of desire for this ministry does not necessarily guarantee that they will be chosen as candidates for the presbytery.

The local leadership should compile a list of those who desire this ministry. This list would be then evaluated by the leadership as to each one's qualifications for presbytery ministry. An approved list would then be finalized of those chosen as candidates.

The approval of those chosen as candidates should be made known to them early enough so that they can properly prepare spiritually for the presbytery meetings. This notification may be made known through the posting of an approved list, through a public reading of the names, or through personal notification.

Those who are not chosen should be told through counseling what is lacking in their readiness for such a ministry. Eventually, everyone can receive this ministry as they become spiritually qualified for it.

A husband and wife should receive this ministry together if they are both believers. If one of the spouses is not as spiritually qualified as the other, they still should both receive this ministry together.

One spouse may desire this ministry while the other does not want it.

The one desiring it should not be prevented eventually from being ministered to by a presbytery. The hesitant or unwilling spouse, however, should not be forced to submit to the presbytery. Wisdom may deem it best to delay it to a later time in certain cases, so that the hindrances and hesitancies might be eliminated through counseling and the subsequent ministry of the presbytery received by both. If someone has an unsaved mate, he or she should also not be prevented on this basis from being ministered to by the presbytery.

Special seating arrangements should be made available for the chosen candidates during the presbytery meetings. The candidates should be seated together in the front rows adequately reserved for the number of chosen candidates. This allows the candidates to be more accessible to the presbytery during the time of ministry to them. The candidates would be instructed to sit in these front seats, and the rest of the congregation would be instructed to leave these seats reserved for the candidates.

The Preparation of the Candidate

The candidate should prepare spiritually for the coming presbytery. It is usually recommended that the candidate fast and pray for three consecutive days within several weeks of the presbytery meetings. The candidate should only have water during this time.

It is best for the candidate to take the time off work for fasting, if possible, so that he can give himself more earnestly to seeking God. The candidate should not jeopardize his job, however.

If a working man cannot fast for three consecutive days because of the need of maintaining his strength, he should fast at least three different days. If a potential candidate is unwilling to spend three days in fasting and prayer, he probably should not be allowed to have this ministry. This approach is not intended as a legalistic stipulation, but rather a guideline required of the candidate to assure a spiritual preparation of him for the presbytery ministry.

Fasting and prayer is not for the purpose of "earning" anything special from God. Rather it prepares the heart to seek God more intently and to have the right spirit to properly receive the prophetic word from God.

The candidates should receive instruction concerning the ministry of prophecy and the laying on of hands of the presbytery. Also they should receive some instruction on fasting both from a scriptural and practical basis.

The candidate should prepare his heart so as to approach a presbytery with no preconceived or presumptuous ideas of what God should speak to him. However, if God has already been speaking to him about certain areas of ministry, he may look for prophetic confirmations to what God has already been speaking to him.

Therefore, an honest searching of one's heart is essential to allow a purity of motivations. Otherwise, the candidate confuses his own desires with God's will and is frustrated and angry when God does not confirm these ideas in the prophetic word to him.

The Responsibility of the Candidate in Presbytery Meetings

The candidate should maintain an intensity of worship and the seeking of God throughout the meetings. He will sit in the reserved front seats and wait until he is called by the local church leadership to come for the ministry of the presbytery.

The candidate will come to the platform and kneel at one of the chairs which is arranged there for the candidates. Usually two chairs are placed on the platform so that a couple may also kneel, each at a chair.

The candidate should lift both hands and begin to worship God either in English or in tongues. As the prophetic word begins, the candidate should immediately cease his worship so as to hear the message from God.

Revelation 2:7, "He that hath an ear, let him hear what the Spirit saith unto the churches...."

Occasionally, no prophetic words will come through the presbytery over a certain candidate. The candidate should not feel embarrased, resentful, or rejected of God. It would rather indicate that the candidate is doing well and that there is nothing more at this time that God would have need to say to him. The presbytery will then just pray over the candidate, blessing him by the laying on of hands.

The candidate must not ask the presbytery for prophetic insight in any particular area of his life. The presbytery will minister prophetically only what God gives them to say. Therefore, regarding those issues that God does not reveal to the presbyters, the candidate should not demand to receive a word.

THE PRESBYTERY MEETINGS

The Scheduling of Presbytery Meetings

The ministry of personal prophecy and the laying on of hands of a presbytery should occur in the local church setting. Such ministry can occur at special meetings, such as camp meetings, if proper oversight of the leadership is present. However, this practice should be the exception rather than the rule. In the church setting, the candidates for a presbytery have properly prepared for these services, and the *whole* congregation is there to witness the prophetic words from God.

Serious problems can occur when such ministry occurs in the smaller home meetings. Usually there is no governmental oversight present to judge the prophetic word and to safeguard against foolish directive words. Usually those who would move in this sphere in a home meeting are novices in the prophetic realm who do not have proven prophetic ministries. This ministry should be reserved for the assembly and the ministry of mature presbyters.

A presbytery may be scheduled as needed by the local church. As new people are added to the church, they will eventually be ready for this ministry after a season of proving themselves within the congregation. Many growing churches of moderate size have one presbytery a year. Some smaller churches may have a presbytery every two years, while some larger churches will have two presbyteries a year. There can be no rule, but each presbytery is scheduled by the leadership as determined by the need within the body.

Presbytery services should be planned well in advance of the desired time to assure proper instruction and preparation of the people. Also many presbyters with mature prophetic ministries have full itineraries which would not permit them to come on short notice.

During the appointed presbytery services, morning services are often scheduled. Those candidates who are single, such as young people, widows, divorcees, and the like, may receive the ministry of the presbytery in these morning services. This allows the evening services to minister to married couples, of which the working husband may be unable to attend the morning sessions.

The Order of a Presbytery Meeting

A presbytery meeting will usually be quite different from the regular order of church services. There is no regular order to a presbytery service. Such a season is a "solemn assembly" (Joel 1:14; 2:15) for the local church. It is a time where the whole church body, not only the candidates, seeks the Lord and presses into God with greater intensity.

Therefore, each presbytery service will begin with a time where the whole congregation is in prayer and worship to God. Although the local assembly may have a regular pre-service prayer time, the time of prayer and seeking God may continue beyond the regular scheduled time until the presbytery in conference with the local pastor feel that it is time to change the order of service and that the spiritual atmosphere of worship is at a high tide.

The presbytery, with the local pastor, will at this time decide what should occur next in the service. There may be a time of singing and worship or the presbytery may enter directly into the prophetic ministry. Sometimes the ministry of the written Word of God will come before the prophetic ministry, sometimes after it, and sometimes it will be omitted from a particular service.

It is good, however, to allow time for the ministry of the written Word in a presbytery service, which will help to keep in balance the primary importance of the written Word of God in comparison with the prophetic word. The preaching of the Word of God should be limited to a short time, approximately a half hour, so as to leave plenty of time for the prophetic ministry.

The Procedures of a Presbytery Meeting

As the prophetic ministry of the presbytery is ready to begin, the local pastor or someone in the local leadership assigned by him will go to the front seats reserved for the candidates and ask a candidate to come forward to the platform for this ministry. The choice is made from the approved list of candidates which the individual should have with him, marking off those who have already received this ministry.

After the candidate has been ministered to with the laying on of hands of the presbytery, he will go back to his seat while another candidate is selected and goes to the platform for this ministry. During this time the congregation should sing songs appropriate for a spirit of worship, and then should enter again into a time of corporate worship.

Someone should be designated by the local leadership to lead in the congregational singing and worship during the time of the exchange of candidates. This individual should be spiritually sensitive and experienced in the leading of worship.

It is proper and of great advantage to record the prophecies for later review by the candidate. In the Tabernacle of David and Solomon's Temple, certain Levites were appointed to "record" the songs and prophetic utterances which came forth (1 Chronicles 16:4). Modern technological equipment has made recording a much simpler task in our day. Usually a microphone is placed on a stand between the two chairs on the platform so as to be centrally located to record the prophetic messages.

It is beneficial for the church to subsequently provide the candidate with an audio tape recording of his prophecies. During the actual time of ministry of the presbytery, the excitement of the moment and the awesome occasion of being before the whole church and revered, mature ministries, can cause the candidate to miss the impact of some of the things God was saying to him. A later reviewing of it can allow God to speak again to the individual.

Some churches also utilize secretarial help to type the prophecies on paper from the tape recordings, since not everyone owns a tape recorder.

Both the typed copy and the audio tape would be given at no expense to the candidate.

The fact that someone has a typed presbytery prophecy is no guarantee of its eventual fulfillment. As seen above, all such prophecies are conditional, and the candidate bears a subsequent responsibility to fulfill in obedience all that God has spoken to him to do. The typed prophecies are never to be considered as authoritative to him as God's written Word.

Some churches keep a permanent, typed copy of the candidate's presbytery prophecies in a file under his name. Thus when the local leadership later counsels with him, the content of what God spoke to him in the presbytery is readily accessible to the oversight to aid in the counseling of the person.

THE RESPONSIBILITY OF THE LOCAL CHURCH IN PRESBYTERY MEETINGS

THE RESPONSIBILITY OF THE LOCAL LEADERSHIP

Responsibility before the Presbytery Meetings

The local leadership bears the responsibility of preparing the church for presbytery meetings. These preparations will be in the following areas:

a. Practical preparations

- The local leadership is responsible for the arrangement and scheduling of the presbytery services and the visiting presbyters.
- They are responsible for the approval and notification of qualified candidates for the presbytery.

b. Spiritual preparations

A presbytery is a time of "setting in" and confirming ministries within the body. It is not a panacea for church problems. Therefore, a local assembly should have evidence of the following corporate characteristics:

- Unity in the assembly.
- A strong flow of corporate worship and the singing of spontaneous praise.
- A church which is strong in regular, corporate prayer.

The local ministry should frequently teach on these vital areas in the church. These characteristics are keys to a strong, body life in the assembly. They should be considered as priorities to be operating in the congregation before the church decides to have a presbytery. If any one of these areas is glaringly weak in the church, the local leadership would do better to delay a series of presbytery meetings and seek to strengthen these important areas of corporate life.

c. *Instructional preparations*

- The local leadership should allow sufficient time for teaching the church as to scriptural instruction about the laying on of hands and prophecy as well as practical instruction as to the functional operation and procedures of the presbytery meetings. (See below for a sample series of handouts which may be used as a teaching guideline to prepare the church for presbytery services.)
- The whole church should be requested to fast one day a week for a full month prior to the presbytery. There should be some teaching provided for the congregation on both the scriptural and practical aspects of fasting.

Responsibility after the Presbytery Meetings

After the presbytery the local church leadership bears the responsibility of shepherding oversight to assist the candidate in the full realization of the prophetic word over him. This might be accomplished by the following means:

a. Counselling

The local leadership should initiate a counselling session in which there is interaction with the candidate regarding his prophetic word. The congregation should be warned publicly not to try to interpret the prophetic words of any candidate. This should be left to the counsel of the leadership. Violation of this guideline by the congregation can bring confusion to the candidate since some people may have differing and conflicting interpretations. The candidate and leadership can prayerfully meditate upon the prophetic word in order that God will make fully clear his will and purpose for the individual.

1 Timothy 4:14-.15, "Neglect not the gift that is in thee, which was given thee by prophecy, with the laying on of the hands of the presbytery. Meditate upon these things; give thyself wholly to them, that thy profiting may appear to all."

Sometimes God gives warnings or stated conditions that need to be reinforced by the leadership. Also, God will occasionally speak to the candidate things which have been previously given in counsel to the candidate. Post-presbytery counsel now allows a follow-up of the confirmation by God of the need of change in the candidate in this particular area of his life.

b. Encouragement

One of the tests that the candidate will later realize is the test of delay. As seen above, it took many years before Joseph's revelation of ruling was realized (Genesis 37–45).

Sometimes the candidate expects the prophetic word to be immediately fulfilled. It usually takes a considerable amount of time, however, as God works into the candidate's life those things which will facilitate the fulfillment of His purpose.

c. Development of the candidate's ministry

The local leadership must take time through counsel and teaching within the assembly to help the people understand the nature, function, and limitations of the various ministries which God has birthed within the body. The leadership should also eventually allow opportunities for the candidate's ministry to begin to operate. However, caution must be exercised not to push or rush someone into a functioning ministry prematurely. This can result in eventual harm to the individual and possibly the whole body.

As a candidate subsequently begins to operate in his ministry, his gift will make room for itself. The leadership must, however, be alert enough to recognize this emerging ministry and channel it into areas which will be fruitful for the whole church.

The Responsibility of the Local Congregation

Responsibility before the Presbytery Meetings

The local congregation also bears a responsibility of preparing themselves spiritually for presbytery meetings. Such meetings are a time for the entire church to receive a fresh visitation of God, not just the candidates.

Therefore, the local church should have one day a week for a period of a month prior to the presbytery services designated as a day of prayer by the leadership. The church facility could be open for prayer at any time on this day, including the evenings (example: 9:00 A.M. to 10 P.M.) for the people to come as they are able. This should be the same day as the church is asked to fast by the leadership. The congregation should gladly respond with diligence to seek God and prepare themselves to hear from Him.

Responsibility during the Presbytery Meetings

During the presbytery meetings the congregation should be open in their spirits to receive individually from God. Although someone may not be a candidate, he can be ministered to personally through the prophetic word over another candidate.

God will speak prophetically in principles regarding His ways and His dealings. Although a certain prophetic word was given over someone else, the Holy Spirit will often cause the true principle of God's ways reflected in the prophetic word to minister to others present in the congregation. Proper spiritual preparation of the whole church allows God to take the prophetic words and to sow them in the hearts of others who were not even candidates.

Also, God will sometimes speak in clear direction through the prophetic ministry of the presbyters to the entire church as a body. The whole church must be ready to hear from God as to the direction that God would indicate to the church at this time.

During the presbytery services, the church has a vital responsibility of maintaining a high level of praise and worship. The prophetic flow of the presbyters, including the depth of prophetic revelation, is in part dependent upon the congregational atmosphere of praise and worship.

Scripture clearly supports the fact that true worship quickens and deepens the prophetic word. God's Word shows that the atmosphere of worship is vital to the prophetic flow. In 2 Kings 3:11–16, King Jehoshaphat desired a prophetic word to give him personal direction. The prophet Elisha was summoned who first called for a minstrel to come. Only after the minstrel played and brought an atmosphere of worship and singing unto the Lord did Elisha then begin to prophesy.

In 1 Samuel 10:5–10, a company of prophets were coming down a road, preceded by those who played instruments and were ministering unto the Lord in worship. Because of the quickening of this anointed worship, even Saul began to prophesy.

There is a danger that a congregation may want to be spectators rather than strong participants in worship in the presbytery services. This is especially true of a church who is having their first presbytery meetings. The novelty of the services causes people to want to simply watch rather than worship God with intensity.

A local congregation must discipline themselves spiritually to continue to press into God in a spirit of praise and worship throughout the services. Presbytery services tend to be lengthy at times, yet the congregation should continue to maintain a high level of praise and worship. Proper spiritual preparation of the congregation is important to assure this discipline of the people.

Responsibility after the Presbytery Meetings

After the presbytery services, there is a tendency for a congregation to begin to relax spiritually and to let up in their seeking of God. When this happens, some of the spiritual blessings which the church has received can be lost.

Although there is a natural easing of the intensity of pressing into God since the whole church will not continue to observe certain days of fasting and prayer, the congregation need not minimize the spiritual blessings of that season by spiritual laxity. The church should be instructed and exhorted to be faithful and consistent in their church attendance and their worshipping and seeking God.

The congregation should continue to pray for those candidates to whom God has spoken during the presbytery season. They must restrain themselves from any prodding of the candidates as to the fulfillment of the prophetic word to them. This would only result in an unhealthy anxiety and frustration on the part of the candidates. As a ministry or a spiritual gift begins to function in the lives of the former candidates, there must be a ready acceptance and spiritual receptivity to the emerging ministry.

BENEFITS OF THE LAYING ON OF HANDS AND PROPHECY BY THE PRESBYTERY

A church should not rush impulsively into presbytery meetings with the laying on of hands and prophecy. Yet, as a church is properly prepared for such a season, there are certain significant benefits and blessings which will be realized by the assembly through these meetings. These benefits are the following:

1. The church will gain a greater realization of each one's responsibility to function in a ministry.

2. The church will receive a greater appreciation for the various ministries in the body of Christ and the need for them.

3. Presbytery services involve a "setting in" of ministries in the local church. These services help each one to find his place in the body of Christ.

4. In presbytery services, the will of God is confirmed to the individual candidate.

5. Presbytery meetings make possible the further development of ministries within the local body.

6. Presbytery services greatly strengthen the lives of individual believers by giving them specialized assistance through prophetic revelation.

7. These services strengthen the whole church in a better understanding of God's ways through receiving the prophetic ministry.

8. The spiritual level of the whole church is raised as the assembly seeks the Lord in fasting and prayer.

9. The church as a whole will receive prophetic direction.

10. There is an impartation of gifts and blessings to individual believers by the laying on of hands.

11. There comes a greater recognition of God's order in the authority of local leadership as overseers of the lives of the people.

12. There comes a deposit of faith in the hearts of the congregation to see God's purposes fulfilled.

While the laying on of hands and prophecy of the presbytery brings such benefits and blessings to the local assembly, this ministry must always be viewed in proper balance. It should be clearly understood that presbytery meetings are not the only way for a believer to discern the will and mind of God. The presbytery is not the only way to receive guidance as to ministry.

The believer should seek God for himself to know God's will and purposes for his life. God is ever ready to reveal His will to the believer (Ephesians 5:17; Colossians 1:9). As the spirit-filled Christian seeks to know God's will, the Holy Spirit will bear witness in his heart as to the divine purposes for his life. A presbytery is not a substitute for the believer seeking God personally or an easy and quick means to know God's mind for a lazy Christian.

The presbytery meetings, therefore, must not be seen as a kind of spiritual "fortunetelling" time where the believer blindly waits to hear something completely alien to him. Rather, as the diligent child of God seeks God and receives direction personally from Him, the Lord will later speak through prophecy of the presbyters to give clarity and confirmation to His will and purposes in order that the individual, the local leadership, and all the local assembly may bear witness to it. The individual believer, with confidence, may then step forward in faith to fulfill God's will for his life with the blessings of the local oversight and the prayerful support of the local congregation.

Teaching Materials for the Local Church

The following outline has been provided as a teaching tool for instruction of a local church in the laying on of hands and prophecy of a presbytery. This outline would be a structure for note-taking by the people during various teaching sessions. The instructor will find the following areas discussed in depth above. This outline may be copied and used as handouts to the local congregation. The above material in this book has been greatly reduced to the essentials and organized below for availability to the assembly.

If the outline below is reproduced as handouts to the local assembly, it is requested that there be no additions or deletions to this material. Otherwise, permission to reproduce it is withdrawn. None of the above material except the following structured outline is to be reproduced.

THE LAYING ON OF HANDS AND PROPHECY OF THE PRESBYTERY

In this day, God has truly been pouring out His Spirit on all flesh (Joel 2:28). The gifts and ministries of the Holy Spirit are now operating in the Church. Each believer has been given a ministry (Ephesians 4:7) and has a responsibility within his own local church to be a "joint that supplies" (Ephesians 4:16).

It is necessary that these ministries be commissioned, confirmed, and set in order in each local church. It is the ministry of the presbytery with prophecy and the laying on of hands which God has ordained to fulfill this vital need.

Prophecy and the laying on of hands of the presbytery was practiced by the early church (1 Timothy 4:14; 2 Timothy 1:6). Soon, however, the prophetic ministry began to vanish. The gifts and ministries of the Holy Spirit ceased to operate, and the church was plunged into the Dark Ages. The laying on of hands and the presbytery became only a ritual.

Since the time of the Reformation, God has been restoring divine principles and truths as well as spiritual gifts to the Church. God has likewise been restoring to the church, prophecy and the laying on of the hands of the presbytery. It is no longer a mere form or ritual, but it is again that through which God gives impartation, confirmation, and blessing.

SECTION ONE: THE LAYING ON OF HANDS

THE SCRIPTURAL CONCEPT OF LAYING ON OF HANDS

The Hebrew Concept of Laying on of Hands

The Greek Concept of Laying on of Hands

THE SCRIPTURAL SIGNIFICANCE OF "HANDS"

Scriptural Terms for "Hand" in the Original Languages

1. Hebrew Words for "Hand"
2. Greek Words for "Hand"

The Usage of the Term "Hand" in Scripure

1. The "Hand" as a Term Denoting Power.
2. The "Hand" as a Term Denoting Authority.
3. The "Hand" as a Term Denoting Placement.
4. The "Hand" as a Term Denoting Strength.
5. The "Hand" as a Term Denoting Consecration.
6. The "Hand" as a Term Denoting Provision.
7. The "Hand" as a Term Denoting Ministry.
8. The Term "Hand" of the Lord."

THE DOCTRINAL SIGNIFICANCE OF LAYING ON OF HANDS

The First Principles of the Doctrine of Christ (Hebrews 6:1–3)

The Doctrine of Laying on of Hands

1. Impartation
2. Identification
3. Confirmation
4. Ministration of Blessing
5. Commission of Ministry

ILLUSTRATIONS OF THE DOCTRINE OF LAYING ON OF HANDS

Illustration in the Tabernacle of Moses

Illustration in the Temple of Solomon

Illustration from Judah, the Redemptive Line

The Laying on of Hands as a Double Portion

SECTION TWO: PROPHECY

The Definition of Prophecy

Old Testament Words

1. Receptive Function
2. Communicative Function

New Testament Word

Propheteuo. "To prophesy."

Prophecy and Preaching

The Distinctives of Prophecy

The Nature of Prophecy

The Causative Aspect of Prophecy

The Conditional Aspect of Prophecy

Prophesy as a Sign of Blessing

The Realms of Prophecy

1. The Spirit of Prophecy
2. The Gift of Prophecy
3. The Office of a Prophet
4. Inscripturation

Mode of Prophetic Revelation

The Mode of Receiving Prophetic Revelation

1. Verbal Revelation
2. Visionary Revelation

The Mode of Delivering Prophetic Revelation

1. Revelation through the Prophets' Words
2. Revelation through the Prophets' Life
3. Revelation through the Prophets' Actions

The Sources of Prophetic Revelation

1. The Holy Spirit 2. The Human Spirit 3. The Evil Spirit

Judging the Prophetic Word

1. Prophecy is Not a Perfect Gift
2. Proving the Prophetic Word
3. The Responsibility of Judging Prophecy

Descriptions of the Prophets

Development of the Prophetic Office

1. The Development of False Prophets
2. The Development of True Prophets

Descriptions of False Prophets

1. Old Testament Descriptive Word for False Prophecy
2. Classes of False Prophets
3. Characteristics of False Prophets
4. Figures of False Prophets

Descriptions of True Prophets

1. Titles of True Prophets 2. Figures of True Prophets 3. The Prophetess

THE FUNCTION OF THE PROPHETIC WORD

The Function of Prophecy in a Presbytery

1. Edification
2. Exhortation
3. Comfort
4. Direction
5. Conferral
6. Confirmation
7. Correction
8. Judgment
9. Equipping of the Saints

Responding to Presbytery Prophecies

1. Proper Responses
2. Improper Responses

SECTION THREE: PROCEDURES OF A PRESBYTERY

THE PRESBYTERS

The Description of a Presbyter

1. The Nature of a Presbytery
2. The Formation of a Presbytery
3. The Preparation of a Presbytery for Prophetic Ministry
4. The Function of a Presbytery

The Function of Presbytery in Larger Churches

THE CANDIDATES

The Qualifications of Candidates for a Presbytery

The Choosing of Candidates for a Presbytery

The Preparation of the Candidate

The Responsibility of the Candidate in Presbytery Meetings

THE PRESBYTERY MEETINGS

The Scheduling of Presbytery Meetings

The Order of a Presbytery Meeting

The Procedures of a Presbytery Meeting

THE RESPONSIBILITY OF THE LOCAL CHURCH IN PRESBYTERY MEETINGS

The Responsibility of the Local Leadership

1. Responsibility before the Presbytery Meetings
2. Responsibility after the Presbytery Meetings

The Responsibility of the Local Congregation

1. Responsibility before the Presbytery Meetings
2. Responsibility during the Presbytery Meeting
2. Responsibility after the Presbytery Meeting

BENEFITS OF THE LAYING ON OF HANDS AND PROPHECY BY THE PRESBYTERY

Notes

1 William Gesenius, *Gesenius' Hebrew and Chaldee Lexicon to the Old Testament Scriptures*, p. 590.

2 Benjamin Davies, *A Compendious and Complete Hebrew and Chaldee Lexicon to the Old Testament*, p. 439.

3 Francis Brown, S.R. Driver, and Charles Briggs, *A Hebrew and English Lexicon of the Old Testament*, p. 702.

4 H.E. Dana and Julius R. Mantey, *A Manual Grammar of the Greek New Testament*, p. 106.

5 James Hope Molton and George Milligan, *The Vocabulary of the Greek New Testament*, quoting *Catalogue of the Papyri in the John Rylands Library, Manchester*, II, 12110.

6 Smith, M.J., "Paranormal Effects on Enzyme Activity," *Human Dimensions*, 1:15–19.

7 Krieger, Dolores, "Therapeutic Touch: The Imprimatur of Nursing," *American Journal of Nursing*, LXXV, 5:787.

8 Tertullian, *On Baptism*, VIII, *The Ante-Nicene Fathers*, Volume III, p. 672.

9 Jennings, William, *Lexicon to the Syriac New Testament*, p. 90.

10 Abraham Heschel, "Laying on of Hands," *The Universal Jewish Encyclopedia, VI,* p. 565.

11 "William Gesenius, *Gesenius' Hebrew and Chaldee Lexicon to the Old Testament Scriptures,* pp. 567–568.

12 "Note Ezekiel 24:25 (margin, according to Hebrew) where *massa* is used in a negative reference but in the same significance of the lifting up of the soul.

13 Gesenius, *op. cit.*, p. 525.

14 W. F. Albright, *From the Stone Age to Christianity*, p. 303.

15 Geerhardus Vos, *Biblical Theology*, p. 210.

16 Edward J. Young, *My Servants the Prophets*, p. 56.

17 Helmut Kramer, "Prophetes Ktl. The Word Group in Profane Greek," *Theological Dictionary of the New Testament,* VI, p. 784.

18 J. Harold Greenlee, *A Concise Exegetical Grammar of New Testament Greek,* p. 43.

19 James Hope Moulton and George Milligan, *The Vocabulary of the Greek Testament, p. 536.*

20 Ibid.

21 On numerous occasions the prophetic formula, "Thus saith the Lord . . .," is used to indicate the prophetic utterance. In the original Hebrew it is regularly found in the past tense (perfect tense), not the present tense. It would be better translated, "Thus said the Lord (to the prophet), indicating the imparting of revelations before the prophet spoke.

[22] Napier, B.D. *Prophets in Perspective*, p. 90. Also see R.E. Clements, *Prophecy and Covenant,* p. 31; and Gerhard von Rad, *The Message of the Prophets,* p. 76; and others.

[23] Thorlief Boman, *Hebrew Thought Compared with Greek,* p. 28.

[24] "Richard C. Trench, *Synonvmns of the New Testament*, pp. 342–343.

[25] Paul's reference in verse 22 in the first clause of tongues being "*for* a sign" syntactically governs in the Greek the parallel structure of the second clause regarding prophecy. In other words, the omission of the word "sign" from being repeated regarding prophecy was because it was understood by the parallel structure as obviously intended there. Even some biblical translations repeat the word "sign" regarding prophecy.

[26] Moulton and Milligan, *op. cit.*, p. 185.

[27] Prophecy is actually the main topic of 1 Corinthians chapter 14, but here contrasted with tongues.

[28] Compare Nehemiah 9:26, 30; Jeremiah 25:4; 26:5; 29:19; 35:15; 44:4; Daniel 9:10.

[29] The word "Son" in reference to Christ in verse 2 is an unique Greek syntactical construction called "anarthrous." This process is used when a writer wants to show some special quality in the named person or object. Here it shows Christ in a special qualitative sense as the climax of revelation.

[30] See John 1:1 where the Word is "with" the Father, Greck "pros," meaning before the face of someone.

[31] Andrew Robert Fausset, *Job-Isaiah*. Volume III of *A Commentary, Critical, Experimental, and Practical on the Old and Flew Testament*, p. axxii.

[32] One does not have to be in a trance to be "in the Spirit." However, one who has had an experience from God of a trance may be properly said to have been "in the Spirit."

[33] F. F. Bruce, *The Epistle to the Hebrews, The New International Commentarv on the New Testament*, p. 1.

[34] Lindsay B. Longacre, *The Old Testament: Its Forin and Purpose*, p. 197.

[35] Hobart E. Freeman, *An introduction to the Old Testament Proplicts*, p. 125.

[36] Francis Brown, S. R. Driver, and Charles Briggs, *A Hebrew and English Lexicon of the Old Testament,* p. 867.

[37] Jude, vs. 12, the King James Version reads "spots in your feasts," which in tire Greek literally should read, "sunken rocks."

[38] Keil and Delitzsch, *Psalms LXXVIII to Isaiah XIV, Old Testament Commentaries,* Volume IV, p. 1380.

[39] The Greek construction is unusual, "...according to the prophecies which went before *on thee...* "This perposition, "on," *epi,* is awkwurd and clearly reflects the idea of 1 Timothy 4:14 where the "laying *on* of hands" finds the suntc prewsition used lit a double *manner*. Paul is clearly thinking of a presbytery with prophecies and laying *on* of hands, all put *on* the subjcct.

[40] Barclay, William. *New Testament Words,* p. 241.

Bibliography

Albright, William Foxwell. *From the Stone Age to Christianity.* Garden City, New York: Nelson Doubleday, Inc., 1957.

Barclay, William. *New Testament Words.* London: SCM Press Ltd., 1964.

Boman, Thorlief. *Hebrew Thought Compared with Greek.* New York: W. W. Nortion and Company, Inc., 1960.

Brown, Francis, S. R. Driver, and Charles Briggs. *A Hebrew and English Lexicon of the Old Testament.* Oxford: At the Clarendon Press, 1968.

Bruce, F. F. *The Epistle to the Hebrews.* The New International Commentary on the New Testament. Grand Rapids. Michigan: Wm. B. Eerdmans Publishing Company, 1970.

Clements, R. E. *Prophecy and Covenant.* London: SCM Press Ltd., 1965.

Dana, H. E. and Julius R. Mantey. *A Manual Grammar of the Greek New Testament.* New York: The Macmillan Company, 1957.

Davies, Benjamin (ed.). *A Compendious and Complete Hebrew and Chaldee Lexicon to the Old Testament.* Revised by Edward C. Mitchell. Boston: A. I. Bradley and Company, 1875.

Fausset, Andrew Robert. *Job-Isaiah.* Vol. III of A Commentary, Critical, Experimental, and Practical on the Old and New Testaments. 6 vols. Robert Jamieson, A.R. Fausset, and David Brown, editors. Grand Rapids, Michigan: Wm. B. Eerdmans Publishing Company, 1948.

Freeman, Hobart E. *An Introduction to the Old Testament Prophets.* Chicago: Moody Press, 1968.

Gesenius. William. *Gesenius' Hebrew and Chaldee Lexicon to the Old Testament Scriptures.* Trans. Samuel Prideaux Tregelles. Grand Rapids, Michigan: Wm. B. Eerdmans Publishing Company, n.d.

Greenlee, J. Harold. *A Concise Exegetical Grammer of New Testament Greek.* Grand Rapids, Michigan: Wm. B. Eerdmans Publishing Company, 1953.

Heschel, Abraham. "Laying on of Hands." Vol. VI of *The Universal Jewish Encyclopedia.* 10 vols. Edited by Isaac Landman. New York: Ktav Publishing House, Inc., 1969.

Jennings, William. *Lexicon to the Syriac New Testament.* Oxford: At the Clarendon Press, 1962.

Kell, Carl Friedrich. Psalm LXXCII to Isaiah XIV. Vol. IV of *Old Testament Commentaries.* 6 vols. Grand Rapids, Michigan: Associated Publishers and Authors, Inc., n.d.

Kramer. Helmut. "Prophets Ktl. The Word Group in Profane Greek." Vol. VI of *Theological Dictionary of the New Testament.* Trans.

Geoffrey W. Bromiley. 9 vols. Edited by Gerhard Kittel and Gerhard Friedrich. Grand Rapids: Wm. B. Eerdmans Publishing Company, 1964–1973.

Krieger, Dolores. "Therapeutic Touch: The Imprimatur of Nursing." *American Journal of Nursing.* LXXV, 5:787.

Longacre, Lindsay B. *The Old Testament: Its Form and Purpose.* New York: Abingdon-Cokesbury Press, 1945.

Mounton, James Hope and George Milligan. *The Vocabulary of the Greek Testament.* Grand Rapids: Wm. B. Eerdmans Publishing Company, 1972, quoting Catalogue of the Papyri in the John Rylands Library, Machester, II, 121.

Napier, B.D. *Prophets in Perspective.* New York: Abingdon Press, 1963.

Roberts, Alexander and James Donaldson (ed.). *Latin Christianity: Its Founder Tertullian.* Vol. III of The Ante-Nicene Fathers. 9 vols. Grand Rapids, Michigan: Wm. B. Eerdmans Publishing Company, 1973.

Smith, M. J. "Paranormal Effects on Enzyme Activity." *Human Dimensions.* 1:15–19.

Trench, Richard Chenevix. *Synonyms of the New Testament.* Grand Rapids: Wm. B. Eerdmans Publishing Company, 1966.

von Rad, Gerhard. *The Message of the Prophets.* London: SCM Press, Ltd., 1968.

Vos, Geerhardus. *Biblical Theology.* Grand Rapids, Michigan: Wm. B. Eerdmans Publishing Company, 1959.

Young, Edward J. *My Servants the Prophets.* Grand Rapids: Wm. B. Eerdmans Publishing Company. 1971.

Additional Resources Being Released

by Brian Daehn and Christian Life Publishing

***Possessing Your Inheritance* – by Brian Daehn**

God has promised us three main things through the Abrahamic covenant (Gen. 12:1–3): the Seed (Gen. 22:17–22, Rom. 13:16; 15:5; 17:4–8, 22:17–18), the Blessings (Rom. 12:3; 17:7,13), and the Land (Rom. 13:15,17, 15:5–7, 17:8–22). This book reveals to every Christian that his/her inheritance has been promised, the giants and obstacles a Christian must overcome to receive their inheritance, and how to offensively possess that inheritance in Christ.

***Dynamics of Team Ministry* – by David Blomgren**

Four vital areas determine the success of a leadership team: the way the team works together, the relationships between the team members, the role of the senior pastor, and the role of the supportive team member. This "how to" book describes the step-by-step process of establishing and implementing a leadership team in any local church.

***Sharpening Your Sword* – by Brian Daehn**

Whether you are just starting out as an occasional speaker, a small group leader, or a well-seasoned preacher, you'll go away from this seminar resource informed, challenged, and empowered to reach new heights in your ministry. You will find Brian's inspirational style of communication to be very uplifting and empowering.

If you would like to contact Brian Daehn, he may be reached at:

www.ChristianLifePublishing.org

Or write to: Brian Daehn

2706 N.E. 164th Ave. • Vancouver, WA 98684